Christmas Eve Stories

by

Patricia Looper

Illustrated by Annisa Estes

Copyright © 2011 by Patricia Looper
Illustrated by Annisa Estes

Christmas Eve Stories
by Patricia Looper
Illustrated by Annisa Estes

Printed in the United States of America

ISBN 9781613791752

All rights reserved solely by the author. The author guarantees all contents are original and do not infringe upon the legal rights of any other person or work. No part of this book may be reproduced in any form without the permission of the author. The views expressed in this book are not necessarily those of the publisher.

Unless otherwise indicated, Bible quotations are taken from The King James Bible.

www.xulonpress.com

To Daniel
who brings me orange juice every morning

Table of Contents

A Word from the Author ix

The Gospel according to Luke
    (King James Version) xiii

The Story of Zechariah 19

Elizabeth's Story 47

The Mother's Baby Story 67

Changes, A Story of Joseph 83

Esther, The Legend of the Innkeeper's Wife 103

Tobel, An Angel's story 121

Samuel, A Shepherd's Tale 137

Simeon, A Story of Faith 149

Letters Home, A Roman Story......................... 165

A Word About My Christmas Eve Stories

Several years ago, while planning the Christmas Eve service for the church I served at that time, the idea of a Christmas story came to me. It was a story that I hoped would appeal to people from six to eighty-six years of age, who would be in the Christmas Eve congregation. The following year, I wrote another story. I've been writing Christmas Eve stories every year since then. Each time I read one of my stories, many listeners suggested that the stories should be published.

Although you might want to read the stories to yourself, they were written to be read aloud. Keep in mind that each story was written to stand by itself. What is written in one story might not be in agreement with what is written in another of the stories. These stories are fictional. But, they are based on the true records, written in The Holy Bible, of the birth of our Lord and Savior, Jesus Christ.

When I was a young girl, for a church program, I memorized the first thirty-eight verses from the second chapter of the Gospel of Luke (the King James Version). That was my first Christmas Eve story. It is still my favorite, so it had to be included in this book.

My thanks to members of the churches in North Georgia that I've served, some of whom were the first to hear these stories: Kincaid Memorial UMC, Faith-Riverdale UMC, Graysville UMC, and Hopewell UMC in Milledgeville. Also, the Morganton Garden Club in Morganton, NC has asked me to read one of my stories every year for several years now. I am grateful to the club's members for the encouragement I've received by their yearly invitation.

To you, my readers, I pray that you have a blessed Christmas season every year and that these stories will entertain you and those with whom you share them. I also pray that those who hear these stories, who don't know the stories of Jesus, will turn to God's Holy Word to learn the truth about him and his great love for all people.

Patricia Looper
Morganton, NC
February, 2011

From the King James Version of The Holy Bible

Luke 2

¹And it came to pass in those days, that there went out a decree from Caesar Augustus that all the world should be taxed. ²(And this taxing was first made when Cyrenius was governor of Syria.) ³And all went to be taxed, every one into his own city.

⁴And Joseph also went up from Galilee, out of the city of Nazareth, into Judaea, unto the city of David, which is called Bethlehem; (because he was of the house and lineage of David:) ⁵To be taxed with Mary his espoused wife, being great with child.

⁶And so it was, that, while they were there, the days were accomplished that she should be delivered. ⁷And she brought forth her firstborn son, and wrapped him in swaddling clothes, and laid him in a manger; because there was no room for them in the inn.

⁸And there were in the same country shepherds abiding in the field, keeping watch over their flock by night. ⁹And, lo, the angel of the Lord came upon them, and the glory of the Lord shone round about them: and they were sore afraid. ¹⁰And the angel said unto them, Fear not: for, behold, I bring you good tidings of great joy, which shall be to all people. ¹¹For unto you is born this day in the city of David a Saviour, which is Christ the Lord. ¹²And this shall be a sign unto you; Ye shall find the babe wrapped in swaddling clothes, lying in a manger.

¹³And suddenly there was with the angel a multitude of the heavenly host praising God, and saying, ¹⁴Glory to God in the highest, and on earth peace, good will toward men.

¹⁵And it came to pass, as the angels were gone away from them into heaven, the shepherds said one to another, Let us now go even unto Bethlehem, and see this thing which is come to pass, which the Lord hath made known unto us. ¹⁶And they came with haste, and found Mary, and Joseph, and the babe lying in a manger. ¹⁷And when they had seen it, they made known abroad the saying which was told them concerning this child. ¹⁸And all they that heard it wondered at those things which were told them by the shepherds. ¹⁹But Mary kept all these things, and pondered them in her heart.

²⁰And the shepherds returned, glorifying and praising God for all the things that they had heard and seen, as it was told unto them.

²¹And when eight days were accomplished for the circumcising of the child, his name was called JESUS, which was so named of the angel before he was conceived in the womb. ²²And when the days of her purification according to the law of Moses

were accomplished, they brought him to Jerusalem, to present him to the Lord; [23](As it is written in the law of the LORD, Every male that openeth the womb shall be called holy to the Lord;) [24]And to offer a sacrifice according to that which is said in the law of the Lord, A pair of turtledoves, or two young pigeons.

[25]And, behold, there was a man in Jerusalem, whose name was Simeon; and the same man was just and devout, waiting for the consolation of Israel: and the Holy Ghost was upon him. [26]And it was revealed unto him by the Holy Ghost, that he should not see death, before he had seen the Lord's Christ. [27]And he came by the Spirit into the temple: and when the parents brought in the child Jesus, to do for him after the custom of the law, [28]Then took he him up in his arms, and blessed God, and said, [29]Lord, now lettest thou thy servant depart in peace, according to thy word: [30]For mine eyes have seen thy salvation, [31]Which thou hast prepared before the

face of all people; ³²A light to lighten the Gentiles, and the glory of thy people Israel. ³³And Joseph and his mother marvelled at those things which were spoken of him. ³⁴And Simeon blessed them, and said unto Mary his mother, Behold, this child is set for the fall and rising again of many in Israel; and for a sign which shall be spoken against; ³⁵(Yea, a sword shall pierce through thy own soul also,) that the thoughts of many hearts may be revealed.

³⁶And there was one Anna, a prophetess, the daughter of Phanuel, of the tribe of Aser: she was of a great age, and had lived with a husband seven years from her virginity; ³⁷And she was a widow of about fourscore and four years, which departed not from the temple, but served God with fastings and prayers night and day. ³⁸And she coming in that instant gave thanks likewise unto the Lord, and spake of him to all them that looked for redemption in Jerusalem.

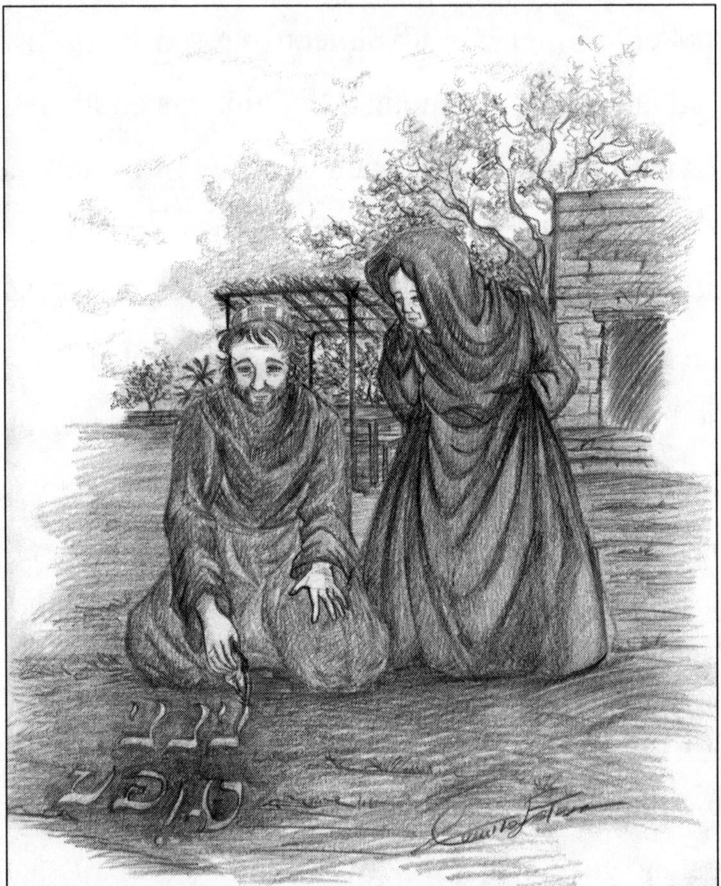

The Story of Zechariah

I'm so much older than most of the priests, he thought, *these might be the last seven days of service for me. This could be my last chance. In all these years that I've come with my clan to serve in the temple, the lot has never fallen to me to take the incense into the Holy Place.*

He watched as one of the priests cast the lots. His heart skipped a beat. He held his breath. Then he couldn't believe his eyes when he saw that he was one of the two chosen to serve that day in the Holy Place. Again the lots were drawn and Zechariah was the one chosen to administer the rite of incense within the Holy Place that evening. Jacob ben Amoz, his cousin and close friend, slightly nodded his head in congratulation.

Zechariah was a respected man. He and Elizabeth, his wife, were moral and righteous people. They lived in a small Judean hill country town, where they enjoyed a good life that satisfied them in almost every way. Their only sorrow was that they were childless; for Elizabeth had never conceived and was now well beyond the years when a woman could bear a child.

On the morning when the lot fell to him, Zechariah remained in the Temple, spending the day in prayer, thanking Jehovah for choosing him for this extra and special rite of service. That evening, Zechariah walked toward the door from the porch where he knew his fellow priests and others would be praying while he administered this task that finally had been allotted him. He was handed the bowl of incense, then he walked through the tall bronze doors.

He paused and glanced around the room. Looking straight ahead he saw the veil that covered the Holy of Holies. Once a year, on the Day of Atonement, the High Priest entered that sacred place. Zechariah was not the High Priest; but he was one of the twenty-four families descended from the sons of Aaron, who served by rotation for seven days in the Temple in Jerusalem. For more than thirty years, Zechariah had served in the Temple, but this was the first time he had ever entered the Holy Place of Incense. It was the first time he had ever beheld the veil that separated the Holy of Holies from the rest of the Temple. Zechariah knew that behind the veil stood the Ark of the Covenant, the most holy relic of his faith.

A feeling of reverence, greater than he had ever known, overcame his entire being. He wanted to lie down the full length of his body in worship before the veil. But, he knew that he had a task to accomplish. His sense of duty was more powerful than his personal, spiritual desires. He walked forward and, following the instructions he had learned and re-learned each time he had come to serve in the temple, he began pouring out the incense. His actions were automatic, even though this was the first time he had actually performed this special and privileged duty. With head bowed, as he poured out the incense, he said the ritualistic prayers that he had memorized.

Looking up from one of the prayers, Zechariah saw a man standing to the right of the altar of incense. *Who is this who dares to enter the Holy Place?* Zechariah asked himself. *Where did he come from? How did he get here?*

Fear etched deeper the lines in Zechariah's aging face. His hands began to shake. His body trembled.

The man began to speak. "Do not be afraid, Zechariah. The prayer request made by you and Elizabeth, your wife, has been heard. Elizabeth will bear you a son and you shall call him by the name,

John. He shall be a delight to you and a joy. Many persons will rejoice over his birth, for he will be great in the eyes of the Lord. He must never drink wine or any strong drink. Even within his mother's womb, he shall be filled with the Holy Spirit. Because of him, many of the children of Israel will turn back to their Lord and God. He is the one chosen to prepare the people for the coming of the Messiah. In the power and spirit of Elijah, he will turn the hearts of fathers onto their children and disobedient persons to the wisdom of the honest ones. He will do all this to make the people ready and prepared for the coming of the Lord."

The still trembling Zechariah, in a voice of doubt and fear, said, "How could what you say come to be? I am old and my wife is also well advanced in years?"

The man then quietly and slowly said to Zechariah, "I am Gabriel, the one who stands before

God, and I was sent to speak to you, and to give this good news to you."

In a sterner tone, the angel continued, "Because you have doubted what I have told you, you will be silent and not able to speak until the day when all that I have said shall happen. For these things will occur in time."

The priests and others who were assembled in prayer and waiting on the porch wondered why their fellow priest was taking so long to fulfill his duties in the Holy Place. They were relieved when Zechariah finally appeared, but wondered why he would not speak to them. They perceived, from his appearance, that something strange must have occurred in the Holy Place. They wondered if he had seen a vision. He tried to speak to the other priests but was unsuccessful, so he gestured to them, but no one understood him.

Upset at his inability to tell his fellow priests what had happened to him, Zechariah gestured for them to follow him out of the inner temple court, through the court of the gentiles, and down the outside steps of the temple. Pausing when his feet touched the dust covered street, Zechariah looked around for a rock with a pointed end. Finding one that satisfied him, he knelt in the dirt to write out the words that the angel had spoken. Before the last word was written, Zechariah heard the disbelieving murmurs and mutters of those who had followed him.

"He is too old... so is his wife... he must have misunderstood... why should an angel appear to him? Messengers from Jehovah would speak to the High Priest?.. I can not believe this... he must be wrong."

One of the priests reached out to help Zechariah as he struggled to his feet. Because Zechariah's speech was gone, the man assumed that he had lost his hearing, too. "Zechariah," he shouted, "you must have misunderstood your vision."

Zechariah, who could hear quite well, gestured to his ear, but the man misunderstood his gestures and shouted louder. The other priests then began to shout at him, too. The shouting became a cacophony of noise, causing Zechariah to cover his ears. He shook his head and once more knelt to the ground.

I can hear you, he wrote. *I heard the angel, too. As you now doubt me, so I doubted him. So, he said that because of my doubt, I would not have speech until these things come to pass. I have lost my speech but not my hearing.*

Once more, struggling to stand upright, Zechariah was helped this time by his cousin, Jacob ben Amoz. "I shall believe you, Zechariah," said Jacob. "Also, I can also see that you are weary. You remained in the temple in prayer all this day and have not eaten since the dawn broke. Come let us go to the inn where we are staying, you need food and rest."

Though he could no longer speak with his fellow priests, Zechariah continued to serve at the temple each day, until his time of service was finished. Although it was somewhat out of the way to his own village, Jacob ben Amoz chose to walk with Zechariah all the way to his home.

While they walked, Jacob asked Zechariah, "Do you want me to tell Elizabeth what has happened to you."

Zechariah shook his head up and down, and then from side to side.

"What are you saying? First I see yes, you want me to tell Elizabeth of your vision, but now I see no that you do not want me to tell her. Stop walking please. Write in the dirt what you want me to say."

Zechariah knelt and wrote; *tell her I was chosen to serve at the altar of incense. Tell her that I had a vision of an angel. Tell her that, since seeing the vision, I have lost the power of speech. That is all. I will let her know what the angel said.*

Seeing the two men approach her home, Elizabeth who had been waiting and watching expectantly for her husband, held out her arms to Zechariah. "Oh, my husband," she said, "I am so glad to see you. I've missed you these many days that you've been away. By any chance did your name get drawn by lot so that you were able to serve in the Holy Place?"

Finally, gently pulling away from her husband, Elizabeth acknowledged Jacob. "My husband's cousin, it is kind of you to visit with us. Please come in. Dine with us. You look well. It has been too long since we visited with you. My husband, you are so quiet. Are you not pleased to be home with me?"

Zechariah turned toward Jacob, gesturing for his cousin to make the necessary explanations to Elizabeth. As quickly and briefly as he could, Jacob told Elizabeth that her husband had been chosen by lot to serve in the Holy Place. He then told her that an angel had come to Zechariah while he was pouring out the incense, and that since that time Zechariah had lost the ability to speak.

In rapid succession, without allowing Jacob the time to answer, Elizabeth said, "What? He has no words? Why has this happened?"

Jacob replied, "That is all I may tell you. Zechariah desires to tell you the rest. Though how he will do that is a mystery to me. He wrote in the dirt all that I have told you. He said that he will tell you more. But, he is unable to speak, and you are unable to read and write. So, I don't know how he will tell you."

Zechariah reached out, taking Jacob by the arm and making gestures for his cousin to speak no more. Jacob shrugged his shoulders, nodded his head, and said, "I will not say a word, my cousin. Your wife asked and I have only tried to tell her. I do this so that she will not worry that you have lost more than the ability to speak."

Zechariah picked up a stick and wrote in the dust.

"Yes! Yes," Jacob said, "I agree that it is up to you to reveal the message from the angel to your wife. I will say no more. It is now time for me to leave.

Despite an invitation to stay and dine, or even remain the night, Jacob declined to stay saying, "I hope to reach my home before the sun sets. Peace to you, to both of you."

Jacob turned and walked back to the road. Watching him, Zechariah moved close to his wife, then taking her arm, he guided her into the house. Closing the door, he embraced Elizabeth, then he gently kissed her in a way that he had not done since they were both young and newlywed.

Because Zechariah continued to hold onto her hand, arm, or robe, even as she served him his evening meal, Elizabeth recalled aloud that her husband was treating her in a manner such as he had not done in many years. That night a spark of young love enflamed the elderly couple.

Early the next morning, Zechariah attempted several different ways to give Elizabeth the news that they were to have a child. The inability to communicate with his wife was quite upsetting to Zechariah. He believed an announcement that a child was to be born to them should be given by himself, not a neighbor, not even a relative.

Later that afternoon, after spending several hours in prayer, Zechariah went to Elizabeth and taking her by the hand he led her out to the front of their home. He then pointed toward the home of a neighbor whose wife had recently had a baby. He gathered his arms together, in a manner such as one would when holding an infant.

Elizabeth was bewildered but finally said, "You want to see and hold the child of Deborah and Jeremiah?"

Zechariah shook his head. Once more he acted as though he were holding a baby, then he pointed to Elizabeth and then to himself.

"I know, my husband," Elizabeth said. "We have both wanted a baby, but it seems that is not to be for us. I hope you do not have in mind to take Deborah's child. That is not the message you were given, is it?"

Once more Zechariah shook his head. Then he bowed down on his knees, with tears of discouragement spilling from his eyes, he looked up to heaven praying that God himself would bring an angel to Elizabeth so that she might know the news he wanted to give her.

Elizabeth knelt by her husband, and though she had not heard the words he prayed, she said out loud, "Jehovah God, please help my husband so that he might give me the message he received in the Holy Place."

After a long time of prayer, the couple re-entered their home, ate a light supper, and retired for the night.

The next morning, having resigned himself to the fact that Elizabeth would one day, by herself, realize that she was with child, Zechariah made no additional efforts to give his wife the news he received from the angel.

Early on the morning of the third day after Zechariah returned home, their neighbor, Jeremiah ben Isaac, came to their door. He told Elizabeth that he was interested in asking Zechariah about his service at the temple. Elizabeth told Jeremiah about Zechariah's inability to speak out loud or to even whisper speech.

Jeremiah offered words of sympathy and was ready to turn away when Zechariah walked out into the yard. He knelt down and with his finger began writing in the dust. Jeremiah read out loud the words Zechariah had written.

"I have lost the gift of speech for a period of time. A miracle will occur and when that happens, my speech will be restored," read Jeremiah. "What is the miracle, Zechariah? Do you know what the miracle will be?"

Again Zechariah wrote in the dust and Jeremiah read the words, "I know but I do not want to say, at this time."

Suddenly, Zechariah stopped writing. He looked up to heaven and then he laughed and began to write once more.

Jeremiah read, "You can help me, Jeremiah. You are an answer to prayer. I want my wife to learn to read and write, so that she can know my thoughts, my needs, and when she has learned to read, she will know the miracle and will tell it to you and to all our neighbors."

"An answer to prayer, am I?" Jeremiah said, questionably. "Your prayer is that Elizabeth learn to write and read? How can I do this, Zechariah? Do you know how this can be done?"

Writing quickly, Zechariah indicated to Jeremiah that he would write the letters and Jeremiah should tell Elizabeth the sound of each letter. Then we will write and tell her some simple words, so that she has knowledge of how the letters form the words. She will gain that knowledge and after a few hours or perhaps a few days, if you will give me the time, I will be able to continue the lessons on my own. I can point to an item, write it down and then Elizabeth will write and then say the word.

Jeremiah explained to Elizabeth all that Zechariah had written. He then said, "Zechariah, you have prayed for a means to commune with your wife. It was at the time of my morning prayers that Jehovah God laid it on my heart to visit with you. Now I know that Jehovah desired to use me to help you. I will not turn my back on this task that Jehovah has given me. I will make arrangements to spend each morning with you and Elizabeth until we are sure she has learned enough to understand the words you want to share with her."

Because she was an intelligent woman who had yearned to read and write, it only took Elizabeth a few days to learn the basic letters and to grasp the idea of written words. Jeremiah needed only to spend a few hours each day with his neighbors before Zechariah was able to take over the lessons. Elizabeth and her husband laughed delightedly together with each new word she learned to write, read, and say. Elizabeth learned so quickly, that she and her husband later agreed that Jehovah had blessed the lessons.

Two of the first words Zechariah had asked Jeremiah to teach Elizabeth were "yes," and "no." That enabled Zechariah to correct Elizabeth if she read or wrote or spoke a word incorrectly. After the words yes and no were learned, Zechariah had Jeremiah teach Elizabeth the words "man," and "wife."

Writing in the dirt on the second day, Zechariah had told Jeremiah to keep the lessons simple. *Do not spend time teaching different ways a word might be written or said. I will teach my wife those things at a later time.*

Elizabeth, who was watching as Zechariah was writing, saw the word wife and immediately pointed to it saying to Jeremiah, "My husband is writing about a wife. I am his wife. Is he writing about me?" Delighted that Elizabeth had seen the word she had just been taught, Zechariah gestured for Jeremiah to read aloud all that he had written.

Finally, the day arrived, actually less than four weeks after the lessons began, when Zechariah knew he could dismiss Jeremiah and continue Elizabeth's lessons on his own. With small gifts and gestures of appreciation, Zechariah thanked his neighbor for all the help he had given them.

Now, alone with his wife, Zechariah knelt in the dirt and wrote the following words,

Angel, spoke, wife, husband, miracle, child, name John.

Elizabeth slowly read and sounded out loud each of the words. Then, looking at Zechariah, she said to him, "Am I the wife of which you write?"

Zechariah nodded yes. Then Elizabeth said, "Before wife is the word angel and then the word spoke. Jacob, our cousin, said that an angel spoke to you when you were in the Holy Place. Next to the word spoke is the word wife, and you say that is me. Then, I see the word, husband. Is that you?"

Again Zechariah nodded his head up and down.

"Did the angel speak to you about me?"

Another affirmative nod, led Elizabeth to the next word. "Now I've come to the word, miracle. Is your loss of speech a miracle? The next word is child. Are you now like a little child in that you have no speech? I don't like that miracle. You have a deep, kind, and gentle voice, my husband. I miss the sound of your voice calling to me from the nearby brook or field. This loss of speech is not a miracle to me."

Zechariah picked up the stone with which he had been writing, *No, no, no*, he wrote. Then he wrote the word miracle and the word child beneath it.

Again Elizabeth sounded out the words. "Miracle and child. A child will cause a miracle to happen?"

Zechariah vigorously shook his head no. The he wrote the word miracle in large letters and he underlined the letters.

"Has a miracle happened, Zechariah," asked Elizabeth.

Zechariah shook his head no, and then nodded yes.

"Husband, I cannot understand a yes and a no coming so close together," Elizabeth said in frustration. Then she began to cry.

Zechariah, who was also quite upset, reached for his wife and held her, wiping her tears away with the corner of his robe.

Finally, Zechariah again began to write in the dust. He wrote, *Husband wife miracle*. Then he made nine slanted strokes in the dirt; then he wrote, *child* and lastly he wrote the word *John*..

Elizabeth read the first three words, then she said, "What word is this? You and Jeremiah did not teach me a word with only slanted marks."

Zechariah then pointed to each mark, and held up all of his fingers and one thumb, with the other thumb folded into his palm. Elizabeth, seeing that the strokes on the ground matched what she saw of her husband's hands, said the word, "Nine."

Zechariah beamed as he nodded yes. He then lovingly placed his hands on his wife's stomach and spread out fingers and thumb. He smiled as he pointed to the word, child.

"Oh, I understand," Elizabeth said, "The angel told you that a miracle child would be born in nine months. What miracle child?"

Zechariah pointed to himself and then to Elizabeth. A puzzled expression appeared on Elizabeth's face; then she said, "Husband, are you trying to tell me that you and I are to have a child? What a miracle that would be, for I am long past the time of child bearing. Zechariah's head nodded up and down, as tears fell from his eyes. But, Elizabeth could see that they were tears of joy. Zechariah raised his head and waved his arms toward the heavens.

As comprehension dawned upon her, Elizabeth fell to her knees. She also raised her hands toward heaven and said, "Jehovah God, if you should desire this from me, even in my old age, I will bear this child. I see that my husband has written the word, John, by the word child, if you desire that this miracle child be named, John, so be it."

Within a few weeks, Elizabeth began to experience the signs of pregnancy. For a while, Elizabeth was ill. Even when she did not feel well, she and Zechariah prayed in thanks to God for the coming miracle. They prayed each morning, and again at noon, and every evening. Elizabeth only experienced the illness that comes in the early months of pregnancy in the mornings. By afternoon she felt well. Her appetite increased so much that she and

Zechariah laughed with joy that she was eating for two.

Six months after Zechariah had lost his ability to speak, during the evening time of prayer, the couple heard the sound of bells from a caravan that was passing near their home. Within a few moments, a voice called out for Elizabeth. When Elizabeth rose from her knees and walked toward the gate of their home. Again the voice called, "Elizabeth, Cousin Elizabeth."

At the sound of that voice, Elizabeth felt the babe within her body leap. Then she saw her young cousin, Mary, who was from Nazareth. Elizabeth immediately knew that another miracle was happening.

Within herself, and by the Spirit of Jehovah God, she had assurance that Mary also was going to have a child, and Elizabeth knew the nature of her cousin's child. Seeing Mary, Elizabeth called to her. The two women were first cousins but several decades marked the difference in their ages. After they embraced one another, Elizabeth told Mary and Zechariah that Mary was blessed. "I know this, because Jehovah God revealed it to me when you called out to me from our gate."

"You, Mary, have been chosen to bear and bring into this world the promised Messiah. The Messiah for whom we have long prayed. We are blessed to have you visit our home."

Then Zechariah and Elizabeth brought Mary into their home where the young woman stayed to help the older couple until their son was born.

On the day of the child's birth many of Zechariah and Elizabeth's neighbors and Mary rejoiced with them. Eight days later, the couple took the child to the temple to be circumcised. The priest was about to name the child Zechariah, after his father, but Elizabeth spoke up to announce that the boy should be named, John.

"You have no relations by that name," the priest protested. "It is the custom to name the first son after his father or another close relative." Then the priest appealed to the still mute Zechariah to correct his wife's mistake.

Because they were inside the temple, Zechariah was unable to write in the dust, so he gestured that a writing tablet should be brought to him; he took the tablet and the writing stylus and wrote these words, "The child is to be named, John." At that moment, while the priest was still looking at the tablet, Zechariah realized that his tongue was free, and he began to speak. He rejoiced. He sang. He danced.

The miracle child was circumcised and named John. A few weeks later, Mary returned to her home in Nazareth.

John's parents raised him in the manner directed to them by Jehovah. During his growing up years, John was known as John ben Zechariah, which was the way sons were called in those time, in that place, where Hebrew was the spoken language; the Hebrew word, ben, means "son of", so John ben

Zechariah means John son of Zechariah. Today, he is called John the Baptist, who was the prophesied forerunner of the Messiah, whom we call Jesus of Nazareth.

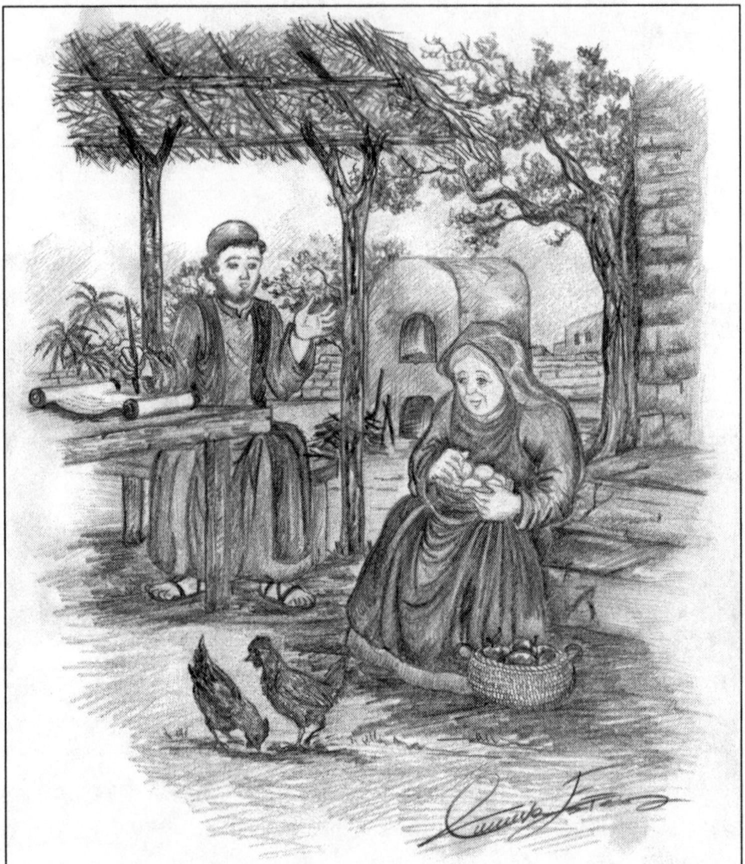

Elizabeth's Story

Blessings be upon you, Theophilus, my friend and colleague. Your letter arrived by courier a few days ago. I rejoice in your interest concerning many of the persons whom I mentioned in my previous epistle to you. I would have responded immediately but had to search for my notes, so much time having passed since I'd written that letter. It takes so long for correspondence to travel between Rome and Achaia. Some of the notes I wrote are quite ancient now, so I make every effort to well-preserve them. They were written at least twenty to thirty years ago. But, I praise God that I kept all of my parchments and scrolls for they surely make the letter writing an easier chore than it would have been had I needed to rack my old brain to recall almost thirty year old memories.

When I began my training as a physician, it became routine for me to ask questions and to make notes of the answers and all other events which I witnessed or heard. To this day that routine has not changed. Perhaps I ask too many questions and surely people do wonder why I always have small pieces of parchment with me. My scratchings probably bother others but they have allowed me, even years later, to write letters or tell someone about people I knew or events I previously witnessed.

Of course, I didn't include in my letter all that I had in my notes, which is a shame because there was so much more that I would have liked to have told you, Theophilus. But some of my written memories would have been superfluous to the reason my previous letter was written.

You have asked me for greater detail concerning Elizabeth, the mother of the baptizer, John. She was a most remarkable and blessed woman. Elizabeth was quite old when I first met her, nearing ninety years. She had outlived all of her siblings, her husband, and most of her friends. In her hometown, a small town in the country, she was regarded with awe, respect and, by those who knew her well, reverence. Her facial lines were characteristic of her age but those around her eyes and mouth signaled kindness and sweetness of nature. Her figure was round and her lap was inviting to young children who loved the softness offered by her ample arms and breast. She looked grandmotherly. But, there were no grandchildren. John, the baptizer, was her only child. He never married and was killed before he reached thirty-two years of age.

You might also recall that Elizabeth's late husband, Zechariah, was a priest. He was a descendent of Abijah, one of the Levites who, centuries ago, had returned from exile to settle in Judah. Elizabeth also was a Levite, a descendent of Moses' brother, Aaron.

Neighbors, who had known both Elizabeth and Zechariah told me that no two people could have lived more godly lives than those two. One neighbor, Miriam the wife of Jacob ben Shem, told me that she had observed that Zechariah and Elizabeth kept all of God's laws.

Miriam said, "They were a blameless pair. Never a shout did I hear them utter. They ate according to the Law. They prayed according to the Law. They kept Sabbath, according to the Law. Yes, a blameless pair, and yet I felt so sorry for them. It was obvious that they loved children. Elizabeth was always baking some goodies and sharing them with the little ones from my home and those of others, as well. And, Zechariah, what a fine priest, a real teacher he was, often stopping his work and telling the little ones stories of Moses, Abraham, or Noah.

Ah, what a love of scripture had Zechariah and how he loved sharing it with the little ones. But, when they both grew too old to have children, did they complain? Not a bit. I knew they had prayed for a child. Elizabeth had mentioned it, more than once, but she didn't complain when the time passed and no child came. No she didn't complain, nor did her husband."

Theophilus, it was Mary, the mother of Jesus of Nazareth, who introduced me to Elizabeth. As I previously wrote, Elizabeth is a kinswoman of Mary's. It was to Elizabeth's home that Mary traveled after the Angel of God told Mary that she, a virgin, would have conceived within her, a boy child. As I previously wrote, Mary was told by that angel that her kinswoman, Elizabeth, was also expecting a child.

As Elizabeth related her story to me, I now share it with you.

My husband and I were betrothed to one another when we were quite young, I had just been weaned and he was less than twelve years of age. Shortly after it became apparent that my body had changed so that I could bear children, we were married. Relatives came from all over the country, from Dan to Gad to celebrate with us. On the day of the wedding Zechariah and his friends came to my parent's home where the ceremony took place, then Zechariah and I led our parents, other relatives and friends to the home that Zechariah had built and furnished for us. It was a wonderful wedding party. It lasted more than three days.

Zechariah had some farm land and some flocks and he was a priest, so that our living was good. Even though our parents had made the decision to betroth us to one another, within weeks after our wedding day, I knew quite surely that Zechariah loved me and I loved him. We were happy and content in our marriage. There was only one problem that we had. Month after month passed and each month there was no sign that we were to have a child.

At first, being childless didn't seem too terrible. We were so happy with each other. But, when a year passed and then a second year, my failure to bear children became a torment to me. I loved my husband so much and I wanted to give him many sons and daughters, but none came. Early in our marriage we had prayed for a son, for every man wants to have a son to carry on his family line, but as the years went by we prayed for a child, not specifying anymore that it be a boy child. We just wanted a child to call our own.

Often Zechariah and I spoke of Hannah, the mother of the prophet Samuel. We recalled her prayers in the temple. So, Zechariah took me to the temple and there we both prayed that God would answer our prayers as he had answered the prayers of Hannah. But, no child came. Finally, when my body disclosed that I would no longer be able to bear a child, we stopped asking for a child when we prayed.

Zechariah often said to me, "Elizabeth, we do not know why God has not granted us the child we prayed for, but someday God will show us the reason and it will be a good one. The scriptures say, 'Who knows the explanation of things?'"

Of course, in later years, when we did have our son, my husband would quote the same book of scriptures, where it says, 'there is a proper time and procedure for every matter.' God, the Father, knew that my body's functions had nothing to do with the time he planned for us to have our son.

Well, I'm getting way ahead of my story, Luke. You asked me to tell you what happened, as I recall it. As you know, my husband was a priest. There were set dates and times when his division of priests, the division of Abijah, was supposed to serve in the Temple. Of course, I only know what Zechariah told me. The division priests draw lots to determine who goes into the holy place to burn the incense. Zechariah was on duty, and he won the lot and went into the holy place of incense, which is just before the Holy of Holies.

Only one priest at a time enters the holy place to burn incense. No other person is in there. So, you can imagine how startled Zechariah was when he suddenly saw what appeared to be a man standing at the right side of the altar of incense. Zechariah finally admitted to me that he was filled with fear. Maybe he thought he had entered the holy place when someone else was there to burn the incense. He never said. The man, realized that Zechariah was afraid and he immediately said, "Do not be afraid, Zechariah." Then the man told Zechariah that his prayers had been heard. He said to Zechariah, "You and your wife, Elizabeth, will conceive and she shall bear a son and you are to call his name, John. He will be your pride and joy. Many persons will rejoice in his birth, for he will be great and wonderful in the eyes of God. Raise this boy to know that he is never to drink wine or other fermented drink. He will be filled with the Holy Spirit, even from birth. Through the work he is born to do, many of the people of Israel will return to follow the ways of God. John will go before the Lord. He will be like the power and spirit of Elijah. The children of Israel, who have disobeyed God, will return to God's ways and become righteous and full of wisdom. Your son, John, is the one who will make the people ready for the Messiah."

Zechariah didn't believe the man at first and questioned him. He said to the man, "I am an old man and my wife is old, too. How can I be sure of what you have told me?"

The man said, "I am Gabriel, the angel. I am often in the presence of God and he has sent me to you to give you this news. Since you doubted what I said and asked questions of me, you will be unable to speak until the child is born, which will happen in the proper time."

The angel kept Zechariah before the altar of incense for a long time. He later learned that the other priests, who were waiting for him, began to think that he had become ill and they were about to pull on the rope that was attached to Zechariah's ankle. The rope is attached so that if a priest does become ill or worse, they can pull the priest's body out of the holy place, thereby not desecrating it by having more than one person in there at a time. Of course, when Zechariah did come out, he couldn't speak. So, the other priests assumed that he had become ill, but he made signs to them so that they realized he had seen a vision.

When their division's time of service was over, Zechariah came home. He made signs to me and tried to tell me what had happened to him; but, I couldn't understand him. You see, Luke, I was not educated and could not read and write. With the help of a neighbor, my dear husband taught me to read, because he wanted to be the one from whom

I would find out about the miracle. It took several weeks for me to learn enough letters and words so that Zechariah was able to write out what had happened to him when he was in the holy place of incense.

Well, Luke, you can imagine how surprised I was to learn that, in my old age, I was to have a child. I kept silent, in those first weeks, and did not tell anyone what Zechariah had revealed to me. Of course, at my age, it was impossible for me to know exactly when the child was conceived. Then several weeks after Zechariah returned home from his temple work in Jerusalem, I began to experience illness in the mornings. That was the sign for me that what the angel had proclaimed to Zechariah would occur.

I did not mind the morning sickness at all. I rejoiced in it. Each day, actually all day long, I kept thanking the Lord for this miracle. I stayed quiet and at rest in my home after that first morning that

I became ill. Zechariah took care of me. He went to the well for our water. He even cooked the meals we ate. When my friends came to see me, I told them that it "seemed that I might soon have a baby. The Lord has done this for me," I said. "In these days he has shown his favor and taken away my disgrace among the people." My disgrace was that I had not given my husband a son during all the years of our marriage.

It was during my sixth month when my young cousin from Nazareth came to visit us. I shall never forget that day or that very hour as long as I live. I had known Mary since she was a babe in arms. Her mother, Anna, though younger than I, was a great friend as well as being a cousin of mine.

Anna was married to Joachim, of Nazareth. Even though there was a distance between us, Anna and I visited together in Jerusalem when our families went up to the Temple for the Holy Feasts and days of celebrations. So, I had seen Mary over the years. I had watched her grow each year since she was born. But, imagine my surprise when I heard her voice in our courtyard. As I walked to the gate the babe in my womb leaped. Oh, such a leap. With that leap I became aware that the Holy Spirit was upon me and in me. I was filled with the Holy Spirit and immediately knew that the Messiah was entering my home. He came in the womb of my cousin, Mary; and, the babe in my womb knew that he was there.

It was a glorious and wonderful day. I told Mary how blessed she was and that I wondered why I was so favored that the mother of the Messiah should come to visit me. I told her how the baby in my womb already recognized that the baby in her womb was the Messiah. Then Mary spoke to me in the words of Hannah, the mother of our prophet, Samuel. The words she spoke were magnificent.

Mary stayed with Zechariah and me until my baby was born. She was a wonderful help to me. Although she was only sixteen years old at the time, she was an excellent cook. Zechariah and I really enjoyed her lentil soup. She would sweep out the floor of our house every morning; while she swept she sang the songs of David. Her voice was soft and the tones I heard were lilting and beautiful to my ears. Often I asked her to sing that beautiful song that many refer to as the eighth Psalm, a song of the Messiah. As my time of expectation increased and the baby grew large within me, I became uncomfortable but always I felt better when I heard Mary sing.

Finally the day arrived when I knew that he would be born. It was not too difficult a time for me. I was too excited to be scared or in pain. Mary called in the mid-wife and asked so many questions of her that the woman thought Mary wanted to train as a mid-wife. Later Mary told me that she was concerned that she might be alone when her child was born, so she wanted to know what to do, for fear that she might have to deliver the baby herself.

Since early childhood Mary had been engaged to a distant cousin, Joseph ben Jacob of Nazareth. Mary had shared with me her concerns about having to tell Joseph that she was expecting a child. "Will he believe that an angel came and told me that God had approved me and chosen me to be the mother of the Messiah?" she asked me. I reassured her that God would take care of her and, if Joseph was to be the earthly father of this child, God would give Joseph the necessary reassurance, so that Mary would not be alone.

Both of us, Mary and I, wondered if we were to raise these special children of God. Well, Luke, we did it. Zechariah and I raised John. Mary and Joseph raised her child. We saw Mary's child many times during his first year of life, they were living in the nearby town of Bethlehem, where he was born. The little boys played together. They were so close in age, only six months difference, you know. Then the tragedy happened. King Herod decreed that all male children two years and younger living in or near Bethlehem should be put to death. Mary and Joseph came to our home in the middle of the night. They told us that Joseph had been warned in a dream to take the child to Egypt and to stay there until it would be safe for them to return to Israel. They wanted us to travel to Egypt with their family.

Because Zechariah and I had not been warned and also because Zechariah was too old for such a trip, we did not go with Mary and Joseph. But, for his safety, that very night I took John and hid in a nearby cave. The boy and I remained there for many weeks, until the soldiers of Rome ceased from killing the children in Bethlehem.

Imagine how happy our family was, many years later, to learn that Joseph, Mary and her son had come back to Israel. They returned to Nazareth to live. After that our two families visited together when we all went up to Jerusalem for the holy days.

Of course, both Mary and I have outlived our sons. Oh, the saddest day in a mother's life is the day she learns that her son is dead. Mary saw her son die. A terrible, cruel and tragic death. I learned of John's terrible death from Peter, a disciple of John's who had become a disciple of Mary's son, Jesus. I'm glad though that my husband was gone before our son's death. Mary also felt about Joseph as I did about Zechariah, that it was better that Joseph died before Jesus began the work that God called him to do on this earth.

Theophilus, this letter probably repeats much that I previously wrote you about John and his parents. Elizabeth was a wonderful woman and it was a privilege to have met and visited with her to hear first-hand about the miracle of the birth of a son that God gave to her and Zechariah. Later, in another epistle, I will write more to you of others whom I came to know whose lives were transformed by God through his son, Jesus of Nazareth.

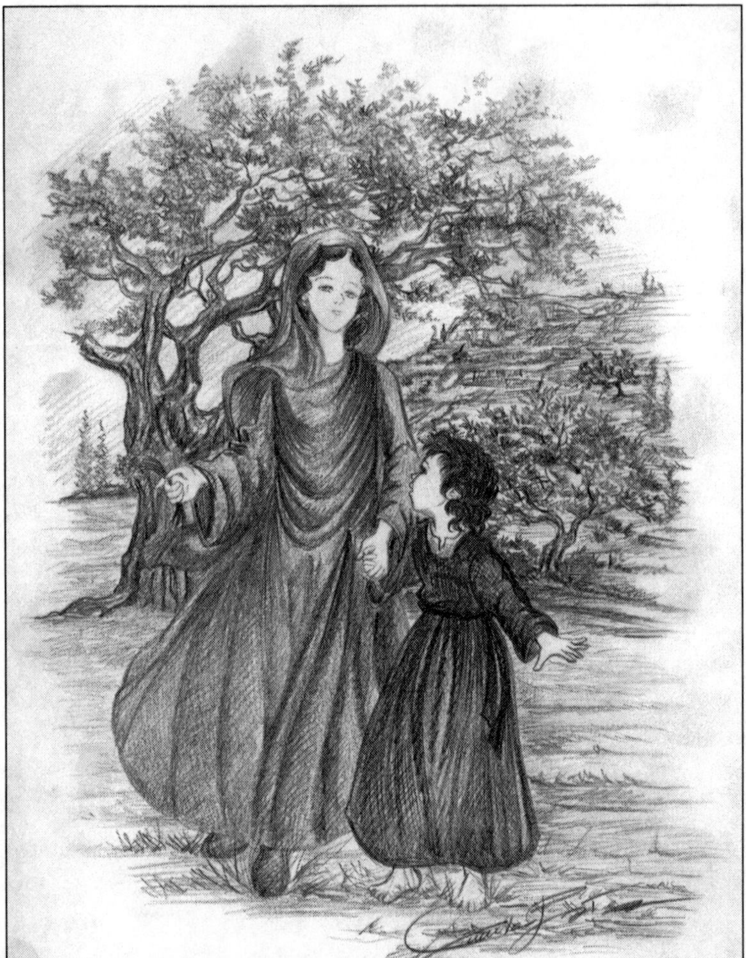

The Mother's Baby Story

I suppose almost all children are curious about what it was like when they entered this world. Knowing that I had asked my mother about my birth, I was not surprised when the "birth" questions were asked of me. I even practiced what I would say. Other mothers have probably prepared themselves to answer those questions, too.

On this Christmas Eve, I can't help but wonder how Mary would have prepared to answer any questions her oldest son might ask. If we could have read Mary's mind, what do you suppose she might have been thinking.

"Perhaps," she might have said to herself, "I should begin at the beginning."

The beginning! What is the beginning? When is the beginning? Where should I begin?

"In the beginning, God..." No that will not do. That is too far back and besides, I really don't understand that part well enough to begin there.

Perhaps the beginning should be when the liar was punished. God said, "I will put hate between you and the woman, and between your offspring and hers; he will crush your head, and you will strike his heel." No, that is still too far back.

Maybe the beginning begins with the prophets. Yes, I could quote Isaiah, Jeremiah, Micah, Hosea, and some of the songs of our faith.

Isaiah wrote, "Therefore the Lord himself shall give a sign, a virgin will conceive and bear a son..." Micah predicted the place of birth when he said, "And you, Bethlehem Ephratha, being the least among the thousands of Judah, out of you shall he come…" Eight hundred to a thousand years before my son's birth, Isaiah and one of the Psalmists knew that kings from the far corners of the earth would bring gifts to him and that they would bow down and worship him. Even the prophet, Hosea, was told to say that when he was a child he would live in Egypt.

All of these statements from the Holy Scriptures are part of the beginning for my son. But to quote those words will not really be my telling my son our story. I have to begin at the beginning as I experienced it. It really wasn't all that long ago either, fewer than nine years have passed since it all began. But, it seems like a lifetime ago for me. My life was so different then.

I was so young, only having passed a few years beyond my first decade. Many years earlier, when I was only a small child, I had been betrothed to my dear cousin, Joseph, the son of Jacob. Joseph's family and my family lived in Nazareth, a town set in a basin, high in the hills, just east of the Plain of Esdraelon, in what is called Lower Galilee.

My father was a farmer, a gentle man of faith, full of love and loyalty to friends and family, alike. Mother was a housewife who could have been the model for the wife of noble character described in the Proverbs by King Lemuel. Together my parents taught me the scriptures, my family's genealogy, and raised me in such a loving home that I delighted in pleasing them by my obedience to their rules and the laws of God.

Often, prior to sleep each night, I would kneel on the floor and thank God for my parents, friends, and the blessings He had given me. As I thanked Him, I also promised Him that I would, with His help, remain pure until my wedding night. I prayed that God would help me to be a good wife to Joseph, when we married. I wanted to be a godly wife like my mother.

The beginning of my son's life, began for me on one of those occasions when I was at prayer. My eyes were closed, but I opened them when I felt a sudden and unexpected warmth. I saw that the room had suddenly filled with a great light. I remember shielding my eyes from the brilliance but still could see through the glow someone tall who seemed to shine like the purest white in that dazzling beam of brightness. I began to tremble in fear.

The man spoke, "Greetings, to someone to whom is given the blessing of the Lord, who is with you. Blessed are you of all women."

I didn't understand what was happening or why this apparition was in my home and speaking to me in such a manner. My trembling grew worse.

Then he said to me, "Do not be afraid, Mary, for you have been so obedient to God's ways, that He is greatly pleased with you. Therefore, God has determined that you shall be the virgin who will bear God's own son, the expected Messiah. A child shall be conceived in your womb. When he is born you are to call his name, Jesus. He will be great and will be called by others, the Son of the Most High. The Lord God will give him the throne of David. He will reign over the house of Jacob, that is Israel, forever, and his kingdom will never end."

My only reply was, "How can this be? I have never known a man in such a way that a child could be conceived in me."

Then the man, whom I believe to have been an angel, said to me, "The Holy Spirit will come upon you, and the power of God will overwhelm you and for this reason the Holy One being born of your body will be called the Son of God. Now hear this, too. Your cousin, Elizabeth, in her old age, has also conceived a son by her husband. This is the sixth month since Elizabeth became pregnant, and many are surprised because she had never had any children. But, nothing is impossible with God."

Overwhelmed with his words of revelation, I answered "Look at me, I am only a humble female. But I am also God's servant, so please let it be done to me as you have said. My heart's desire is to be always obedient to God."

The next morning, my parents and I decided that I should visit Elizabeth, to help her in the final months of her pregnancy. I left Nazareth with the next caravan and stayed with my cousin until her son was born and I could see that she was well enough to handle both her household responsibilities and the care of her son.

By the time I returned to Nazareth, my body was beginning to show the signs of my pregnancy. Of course, the clothing we women wear is loose and that gives us coverings of modesty. So, I knew that I had to tell Joseph what had happened to me.

I thank God that Joseph was the man chosen for me by my family. Joseph is such a good man. He works with his hands and they are large and rough, even though he is the gentlest of persons. When people are talking, Joseph really listens. You can look at him and see him contemplating what is being said. By the expressions which cross his face, one can almost see that many thoughts are being turned over and around in Joseph's mind.

In Israel, an engagement is binding both upon the couple through the civic laws and through the laws of our Jewish faith. Upon being told that his betrothed was expecting a child, most men would ask that the engagement be canceled; which is called a divorce. Of course the reason for the divorce would have to be stated to the local rabbi or even to the Temple Priest. The custom in our country is such that when it is discovered that an unmarried woman is no longer a virgin, the divorce is granted and the woman is stoned to death.

Explaining a miracle, a visit from an angel, and the work of the Holy Spirit really is the most difficult event one person can attempt to describe to another person. Planning what to say and how to say it is challenging. Expecting the listener to understand and believe the miracle has to be left in God's hands. So, I prayed that Joseph would believe me. I said to God, "This is your child. Help me to tell Joseph. Put the right words in my mouth. Let Joseph understand that I am telling the truth."

One afternoon when I knew Joseph was finished with his day's work, I invited him to walk with me. We strolled through the dusty streets of Nazareth, out onto the hills which surround the town. Sitting on the edge of a grassy overhang, we looked down upon the wide and beautiful plain below. Summer blazed around us in the beauty of the flowers, the fields of grain, and the green pastures where shepherds were grazing their flocks. And so, I told Joseph about the angel's visit.

Joseph listened. He didn't say a word. When I finished my strange tale, he stood up and helped me to my feet. Silently we walked back into Nazareth, and Joseph escorted me to my door. Declining, with brief words of thanks, my mother's invitation to dinner, Joseph left.

Early the next morning my family was awakened by a soft knock at our door. It was Joseph. He entered the room, took my hand in his and said, "I look forward to having you as my wife, blessed woman." And so, shortly after that time, he took me home as his wife. But, until the child was born, we had no union such as a husband and wife expect to have when they marry. Joseph was celibate and I remained a virgin.

At that time, our land was ruled by a man called Caesar Augustus, who lived in Rome, a country quite distant from ours. Caesar sent messengers to his governors that a census should take place, so that all of the male citizens of the Roman Empire could be taxed. Each man was to go to the town of his ancestors to register for the census. Joseph and I were both descended from David, an ancient and great king in our land. So Joseph needed to register at Bethlehem, for Bethlehem is the town of David.

The time of my delivery was so near and Joseph did not want to leave me. Then we both remembered the scripture of Micah, the prophet, who wrote that out of Bethlehem would come for God one who would be ruler over Israel. Then Joseph and I knew that God was using this census of Caesar's as a means to insure that the Messiah would be born in Bethlehem. So, Joseph and I both knew that it would be alright for me to travel to Bethlehem, which was a three day walk from Nazareth.

The town was so crowded when we arrived in Bethlehem. Joseph had bought a donkey for me to ride, but I was still weary and looking forward to the privacy and comfort of a room at a local inn. However, the inns were all crowded. We couldn't find a room anywhere. Finally, through the kindness of one proprietor, we were given some space in his stable, which was actually a large cave in a hill behind the inn.

I suppose it was the jostling of the donkey I rode. Even as Joseph helped me from the donkey's back, there was no doubt in my mind that my child would soon be arriving. I lay down in some fresh hay which the innkeeper had spread out for us. I tried not to groan but Joseph could tell I was in pain. He ran to the inn, inquiring for a midwife. Within a few short hours after our arrival in Bethlehem, my son was born.

During the last months of my pregnancy I had woven some blankets and cloths for the child I was carrying. When the midwife laid my son in my arms, she had already wrapped him in some of those cloths. The weariness I had felt when we arrived only a few hours earlier had left me. Now, although physically exhausted, I was excited, too. I unwrapped the blankets and counted each precious finger and toe. I looked at his ears and his nose and marveled at the depth of brown in my baby's eyes. He seemed to see me and I am sure he smiled at me. When Joseph reached out to touch him, one of the baby's little hands latched onto Joseph's smallest finger and held it tight. And, Joseph and I laughed in delight at this special gift which had been given to us.

While we laughed, a great and shining light began to fill the cave and the courtyard which connected the stable to the inn. We were surprised to see the light but discussed the fact that from this moment till we were no longer necessary to this child, many happenings would surprise us, and that we should meet each incident with the reverence God's own son deserved.

That very night, shepherds arrived and knelt down to worship him. When he was still quite young, only a toddler, kings from foreign lands came and brought him gifts. In a dream, an angel spoke to Joseph, telling him to take me and the child to Egypt, for the child's life was in danger.

Later, while we were in Egypt, in another dream, Joseph was told that it would be safe for us to return to Galilee. We came back to Nazareth, and this is where we have made our home. It is a good place to raise a boy. Jesus loves running through the hills that surround our town. He is a good boy and someday soon he might say to me, "Mother, what was it like when I was born?"

So, now I have rehearsed the story from the beginning and I know, with His Heavenly Father's help, I can tell it to him, from the beginning. Although, bearing in mind who he is, my son might know more about the beginning than I ever have known.

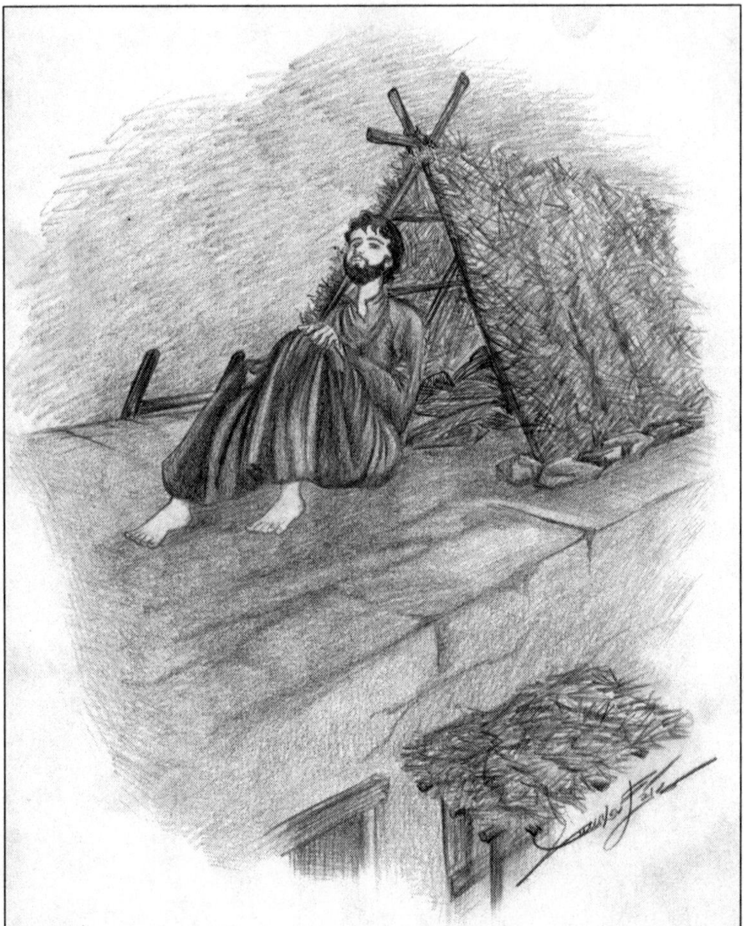

Changes

Holding tight to the donkey's halter, the man walked slowly down the mountainside. He was not pulling on the halter; he held it tight, so that the donkey would not stumble on the rocky path. The young woman on the donkey's back smiled as she gazed down at the man.

He is so kind and good, she was thinking. *I am safe with him.* She then sent a silent prayer of thanks to God for giving her a good, kind, and thoughtful man, to be a father for her expected son. *He truly is a man of God*, she said to herself. *He has been with me through all the changes that have taken place in my life. I am so blessed to have Joseph by my side.*

Who was this man, whom the woman so obviously cared for and respected? His name was Joseph.

Joseph lived in this world hundreds, nay, thousands of years ago. The world was less complicated in those times. A man could live in the same town for all of his life. He could follow in his father's footsteps, as a farmer, a shepherd, or as a craftsman. In those times, a man might never travel even a few miles from his place of birth. Life was predictable and a man knew what to expect from one day to another.

The town in which Joseph lived was called Nazareth. Nazareth is located at the top of a very high hill, in the country of Israel. The outside world did not have much of an effect upon Nazareth and its citizens. Joseph respected the traditions of his faith and his heritage. He was content.

When he was a youth, the parents of Joseph betrothed him to the daughter of a neighbor. Her name was Deborah. Joseph was seventeen years old at the time of the betrothal and Deborah was twelve. The betrothal was acceptable to Joseph and he was pleased when his father negotiated a fair bride price that his family would pay in exchange for Joseph's marriage to Deborah. The betrothal took place in front of witnesses. Joseph knew that he and Deborah would be married within a few years time. Joseph was happy to follow in the tradition of his family, his village, his faith.

Change came to Joseph's life when a terrible disease spread through the village of Nazareth. It struck Deborah and both of Joseph's parents. Within a few weeks, Deborah died. Although Joseph's father and mother survived for a few years, they were never in good health after that time. Joseph became the sole support for his family.

He worked with his hands. In future years people would say that Joseph was a carpenter, and that was true. But, in a land where wood was scarce, the craftsman in Joseph enabled him to also work in stone. He earned a living by chiseling the artistic stone work that decorated buildings in the nearby town of Sepphoris. After Sepphoris was designated the administrative center for that area of Galilee, the building trade became an economic blessing to workers from nearby towns such as Nazareth.

Early each morning Joseph walked three miles northeast to Sepphoris, returning home each afternoon, weary but pleased with his day's work. *I'm always facing the sun,* he thought. *What a pleasure it is to walk in the shining glory of the Creator's sun each morning and evening.*

Many persons in the town of Nazareth experienced changes in their lives by the disease that had taken Deborah's life. One of those persons was a young girl by the name of Mary.

Mary was the daughter of Joseph's cousin, Heli, a descendent of King David. Realizing that Heli was older and in ill health, Joseph decided to claim his position as kinsman-redeemer. It is the responsibility of the kinsman-redeemer to claim the land of a deceased person who has no heirs. At the same time, the kinsman-redeemer also is to pay the debts and care for the female family members of the deceased. By claiming his position, and betrothing himself to Mary, while Heli was still alive, Joseph knew he would greatly relieve his cousin from worrying about Mary and her mother, Anne.

In Israel, in those long-ago times, it was not unusual for a betrothed couple to occupy the same home. By the time Joseph and Mary were betrothed, his parents were deceased. With no family and a small home, shortly after the betrothal was sanctified by the village priest, Joseph moved his few possessions into the home of Heli and Anne. Because Mary was so young, Joseph treated her as a brother would a younger sister. Heli, Anne, and Mary slept in an area above the ground floor of their home, where the few goats owned by the family were bedded down for the night. Joseph made his bed on the roof of the home, where he built an enclosed sleeping area for himself that protected him from the elements.

Mary was almost fourteen years old when her father, Heli, succumbed to the various ailments that had long troubled his body. Anne and her daughter were relieved of the daily care they had been giving Heli, but his death did not deprive them of the necessities of life. Although Anne missed her husband and Mary grieved for her father, life in their small home in Nazareth suffered no other change. Joseph had been supporting the family for many years and that continued. It did not occur to Joseph, Anne, or Mary that life would change much in the near or distant future.

Days, months, and almost a year passed. Each season brought some slight change, but overall, life seemed constant.

It was Mary who experienced the next life changing event. It occurred one night in the sixth month of the year. Mary was asleep when a rush of wind blew aside the robe that she used as a cover. Opening her eyes, she was astonished when a brilliant light flooded the room. Glancing at her mother, Mary was surprised that the wind and the bright light hadn't awakened Anne. Suddenly there appeared in the room a being who spoke to Mary.

The being was an angel and he said, "Greetings to one who has received honor. The Lord is with you. Blessed are you among women."

Mary was both confused and terrified at the bright light, the sudden appearance of a stranger, and at the words she heard from him.

The angel said to her, "Do not be afraid, Mary. You have found favor with God. A child shall be conceived within you. The child will be a boy, and you will call his name, Jesus. This Jesus will be great. This Jesus will be the son of the Most High. The Lord God will give Jesus the throne of your forefather, David. He will reign over the house of Jacob forever, and his kingdom will never end."

Regaining some composure, Mary said, "How can this be, since I have never known a man in the manner that a child could be conceived within me?"

The angel, replied, "The Holy Spirit will come upon you, and the power of God Most High will overshadow you, so that the one to whom you give birth will be called the Son of God. You will know that this is true because your cousin, Elizabeth, the wife of Zechariah, is also bearing a child, conceived by her husband, even in their old age. Elizabeth was thought to be barren, but she is now six months along. In three months she will have a child. This is because nothing is impossible to the Lord God.

Mary was astonished, but she replied, "I am a servant of the Lord God. May it be to me as you have said."

When he heard Mary's words, the angel went away as suddenly as he had appeared. Anne had slept through all that had occurred.

Early the next morning, Mary related to her mother all that had taken place in their room the previous night. Anne was a woman of great faith but the account of such strange events were so unbelievable that she could not grasp much of what her daughter said to her.

"How could Elizabeth, who has been barren all her life and who is decidedly past the age of child bearing... how could she be with child?" Anne asked Mary.

"I do not know," Mary replied. I recall the stranger saying that with God nothing is impossible. Although I do not understand any of this, Mother, I believe I should go at once to the home of Zechariah and Elizabeth. If what the stranger told me is true, than Elizabeth, being six months along, will verify for me all that was said."

Reluctantly Anne agreed. She allowed Mary to leave Nazareth with a group of neighbors who were traveling to Jerusalem. Their travels would take them through the town in Judea, where Zechariah and Elizabeth lived. The neighbors were leaving Nazareth that day and Mary quickly bundled up a few belongings, and set out on the journey to visit her cousins.

That evening, when Joseph arrived home from his work in Sepphoris, Anne explained to him that Mary had decided to travel to Judea to visit with cousins. She did not reveal to Joseph anything that Mary had told to her about the bright light, the stranger, and the message the stranger had given Mary.

The neighbors who traveled to Jerusalem returned to Nazareth, in a few weeks with news that Mary desired to remain with her cousins, Elizabeth and Zechariah, until the birth of their child.

Mary remained with Elizabeth, Zechariah, and the new-born baby, John, until Elizabeth was well enough to care for her family without help. Aged as she was, it took longer for Elizabeth to recover from the birth of John, than it would have for a younger woman.

When Mary returned to her home in Nazareth, she was almost five months pregnant, and the sickness that often comes with pregnancy was upon her, not just in the morning, but sometimes at night, too. The journey home was long and wearying for her. She arrived in Nazareth a few hours before the time of the Sabbath.

Anne, with a mother's loving care and understanding, welcomed her daughter with open arms. That her daughter was tired did not go unnoticed either. Anne gave Mary some warm soup and bid her go to the sleeping loft. When Joseph came home from work, he was pleased to hear that Mary had returned and that she would see him the next day.

"She has something to speak about with you, Joseph," Anne said. "Some changes have taken place. I hope you will listen to all that she tells you, before you judge her words in any way."

It was mid-day when Joseph returned from the Sabbath services at the local synagogue. Anne retreated to the roof-top so that Mary could speak privately to her betrothed husband, Joseph. When Joseph entered the room, Mary was seated on the bare ground floor of their home. She indicated that Joseph should sit, also.

As he sat down, and before Mary could say a word, Joseph said, "You do not have to say anything to me, Mary. I should have arranged for our wedding several months ago. I wanted to give you and Anne time for mourning your father. Tomorrow, I will make the arrangements with the village priest. You and Anne will want to invite all of your relatives, even those who live a distance from Nazareth. Time will be needed for that. Shall I tell the priest that the wedding is to take place in two months, on the third day of the week? That will give everyone a day or two to walk here after the Sabbath and time to return home before the next Sabbath. The wedding feast shall last two or three days, for those who do not have to travel a long distance. I have saved for our wedding; we shall have a grand feast. Is that all you wished to speak about with me?"

"No, Joseph," Mary replied, "I did not intend to make wedding plans with you. I have something to tell you. What I have to say could be very difficult for you to hear and believe. However, you must know that what I am about to tell you is the truth."

In a quiet voice, Mary told Joseph about the rush of wind, the light that had flooded her room, the stranger, and all that he had said. "I know this is difficult to hear and believe, Joseph," she said. "I was not sure, myself, until I arrived at the home of Elizabeth and Zechariah.

"When I entered their home, Elizabeth, in a loud voice, said to me, 'blessed are you among women, and blessed is the child you will soon bear. I do not understand why I am favored, that the mother of the savior should come and visit in my home? As soon as I heard you call out a greeting, the baby in my womb leaped. It was a leap of joy, for the babe I carry knows the voice of the mother of the son of God.' When Elizabeth said that and told me that she was with child, she, who was barren and many years beyond the time when a child could be conceived upon her... when I heard that, I knew that the stranger who spoke to me really was a messenger from God most high. I knew then that the message the stranger gave to me was truth."

Leaning forward, Mary placed both hands on the ground, pushing herself into a standing position. Joseph looked up at her and was astonished when Mary pulled her robe close to her body, revealing her figure. Joseph did not say a word. He just got up and left the house, returning to the local synagogue, where he remained in prayer. Evening came and when Joseph was sure that Mary and Anne would have finished their dinner and retired for the night, he made his way home, climbing to his sleeping room by the stairs built into an outside wall of the house.

Joseph did not want to expose Mary to the disgrace that would occur if he went to the town fathers and the local priest and reported that she was pregnant, even though he had never known her in a husband-like manner. *I thought she was a virgin. I never touched her*, he said to himself. *I do not want to know who the man was who did this to her. But, I will have our betrothal quietly put aside. It will be as though it never was. Mary can return to the home of her cousin in Judea, and no one in Nazareth will know what she has done.*

During that night, while he slept, Joseph had a dream in which a messenger from God, an angel, appeared and said, "Joseph, son of David, do not be afraid to take Mary as your wife. The child that Mary will bear really is the son of God Most High. The Holy Spirit overcame her and the child was conceived. You are to give the child the name of Jesus. He will be a savior for all mankind. He will save them from their sins. All of this has taken place to fulfill the words of the ancient prophets. Isaiah, the prophet, said 'the virgin will be with child and will give birth to a son and they will call him Emmanuel, which means God with us.' Mary is the virgin chosen by God to bear this Savior."

Joseph awoke from his dream. He called out to Mary and to Anne. When they responded to his call, he went down to the lower floor of the house and told them about his dream and that he was going to make Mary his wife. We will have the wedding just as I described it to you, Mary."

Changes continued to affect the lives of Joseph and Mary. A few days after Mary's return home,

Anne fell, hitting her head. She died just a few weeks before the wedding was to take place. The wedding was postponed for the time of mourning. Even a shortened time of mourning should last at least three months. Mary and Joseph agreed that a season of the year should pass before Mary could put off the clothes of mourning in exchange for a wedding robe.

The season of mourning was almost over, and Joseph once again sought out the priest to make plans for a wedding. It was not to be the grand, three day time of feasting, such as he had described to Mary several months earlier. A quiet wedding with their closest neighbors invited, and a wedding feast to last only a few hours. The day that Joseph was to speak to the priest another change took place. Notice was brought to Nazareth that the Emperor, Caesar Augustus, had determined that a census should be taken of the Roman Empire. Each person was to return to the town of the forefathers of his family.

Joseph, like Mary, was of the family of David. The town of David is Bethlehem. Joseph could have registered for himself, but he did not want to leave Mary alone while he journeyed to Bethlehem. The priest was unable to perform a wedding on short notice, so Joseph purchased a donkey, then he and his betrothed wife set out for Bethlehem.

Holding tight to the donkey's halter, Joseph walked slowly down the mountainside. He was not pulling on the halter; he held it tight, so that the donkey would not stumble on the rocky path. Mary smiled as she gazed at the man.

He is so kind and good, she was thinking. *I am safe with him.* She then sent a silent prayer of thanks to God for giving her a good, kind and thoughtful man, to be a father for her expected son. *He truly is a man of God*, she said to herself. *He has been with me through all the changes that have taken place in my life. I am so blessed to have Joseph by my side.*

She gave birth to the boy in Bethlehem. Joseph was his earthly father. They called the boy, Jesus. Jesus came into the world to change it.

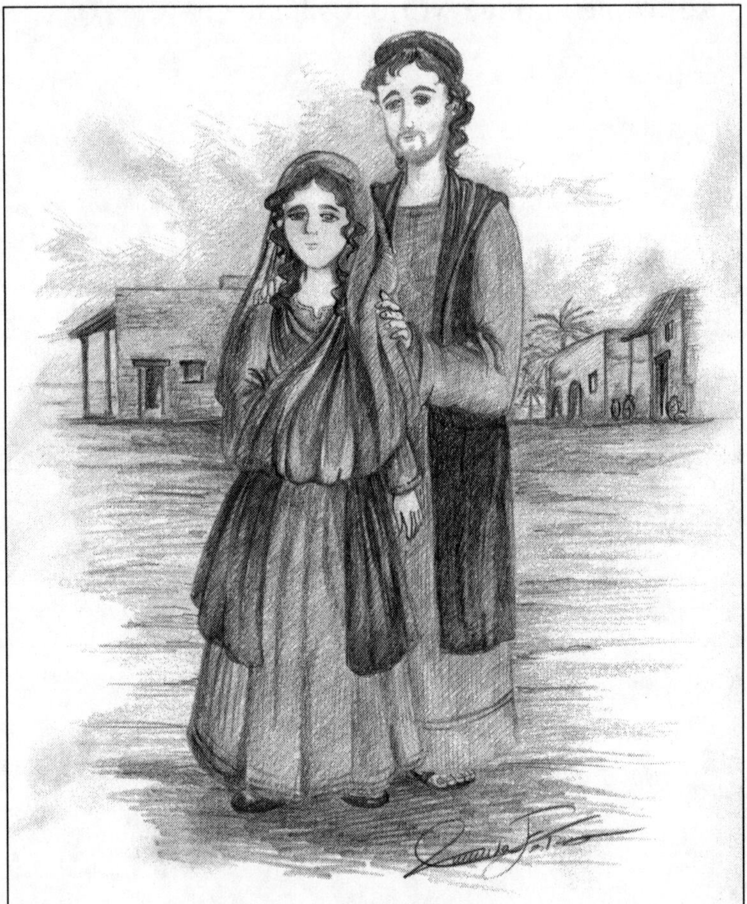

Esther, The Legend of the Innkeeper's Wife

Christmas Eve is such a good time for story telling, and I've been wondering, dear ones, have you ever heard the legend of the Innkeeper's Wife?

What? You haven't?

Well, sit back, relax and listen to this tale.

You probably think, since this is Christmas Eve, that this story begins on that particular Christmas Eve that we read and sing and talk about so much. Well, you would be wrong. This story begins about 30 years earlier than that first Christmas time. However, our story does begin with a birth.

A little girl was born.

She was the first child born to Jabez ben Nebat and his wife, Elisheba. Elisheba was greatly disappointed when the mid-wife announced that the child was a girl.

As she glanced more fully at the little girl, the mid-wife suddenly gave a shriek, thrust the child into her mother's arms and said, "Here, you clean her off, if you want to, I won't touch her again. I'm sorry I assisted at this birth. This isn't my doing."

The mother looked to see what was wrong and discovered that her daughter's right arm was misshapen. It was crooked and smaller than the left arm. The mother immediately began to cry and wail the sorrow she felt when she saw her less than perfect child.

Jabez came running into the house when he heard his wife's cries of woe. He also was devastated when he saw that Elisheba had given birth to a *disfigured, female* child. A double punishment from God, as far as Jabez was concerned, and he too began to wail in sorrow.

It was the grandmother, Jabez's mother, who saved the little girl. She went to her son's home as soon as she heard news of the birth. That news had rapidly spread through the small village along with the running feet and loose tongue of the quickly departing mid-wife. The mid-wife, not being one of those persons who could keep a secret, much less was she a person who could resist the telling and re-telling of a birth such as she had just experienced.

Elisheba wanted nothing to do with her daughter, but the grandmother bathed the little girl and wrapped her in the previously prepared swaddling cloths. She sat on the floor and rocked the child back and forth in her arms, crooning to her and murmuring sweet words in her ear. She was overjoyed that the baby was a girl. Her only child had been a son but, as far as the grandmother was concerned, there was no disgrace at all in having a girl. "You are a sweet, precious child," the grandmother said. "I will love you and care for you, and every day I will tell you how beautiful you are....as beautiful as Esther, the queen who saved our people many, many years ago.

The grandmother insisted that her daughter-in-law feed the child, but she took the unwanted little girl home between feedings and she and the grandfather raised the girl as their own. They called the child, Esther.

Esther was not physically beautiful as was the queen for whom she was named. But, the love and teachings she received from her grandparents were such that Esther grew to be a kind, gentle, and loving little girl. When she was still quite young the grandfather let it be known that he would give, as a dowry for the girl, ownership in his business. The grandfather owned an inn. It wasn't too long after hearing about such a generous dowry that one of the village families brought to the grandfather's attention their youngest son, Josiah, to be formally betrothed to Esther.

Josiah, as the youngest son, would not receive much of an inheritance from his father, so this was a very favorable arrangement for Josiah's family.

After all the formalities and legalities were attended to, the betrothal took place.

As the two children grew, the grandparents gave each of them more and more responsibility in the activities involved with running an inn which was close to the main highway on the road from Jerusalem to Egypt.

Esther was taught by her grandmother to handle most tasks with the use of her healthy left arm and hand. Esther learned, at a very early age, to keep her misshapen right arm tucked away inside her robe. That prevented others from being offended by the sight of that withered and crooked little limb, and it also saved Esther from being taunted and teased by the village children. Though, as they grew older, the other children soon learned that teasing Esther meant they had to deal with the swinging fists and kicking feet of Josiah, who quickly came to the rescue of his little playmate.

Esther and Josiah were grateful for their betrothal when they realized they loved each other, and an early marriage took place shortly after each of the young persons had displayed signs that they had attained adulthood.

Because they had been raised at the inn, they sadly but expertly took over the running of the inn when the grandparents passed away. Esther and Josiah lived a mostly uneventful life as excellent hosts to weary travelers who stopped at their inn. Theirs was an adequate living for which they thanked God. They contributed to the upkeep of the temple in Jerusalem and Esther was especially grateful to God for the life he had given her despite the disadvantage with which she had been born. Esther began and ended each day down on her knees thanking

God for providing her with loving grandparents, a good husband, and the inn for their livelihood. Esther's only regret was that she and Josiah seemed unable to have children, and she often prayed that God would grant her the desire of her heart, that she and Josiah should have a child.

The years passed quickly and smoothly for Josiah and Esther. Business was never too much but was always steady at their inn.

Then the Roman Emperor, Caesar Augustus, decided that he wanted to tax all the citizens of the empire he ruled. In order to tax them, he had to know how many persons there were in the Roman Empire. Therefore, he put out a decree that all the people should be counted. The counting, called a census, was to be done in each person's hometown; everyone was to return to the town of his ancestors to be numbered there with the rest of his family. The inn which Esther and Josiah owned was in the town of Bethlehem, which was the city of David, and

David was a son of Jesse, and Jesse had fathered eight sons. As the descendants of Jesse returned to Bethlehem, the inn filled up and soon was overcrowded with distant cousins each chanting his genealogy as they all tried to discover how they were related to one another.

Josiah rented out every cubicle of space in the inn, even moving his and Esther's belongings into a small storage area close to the outside gate. Eventually people were offering Josiah and Esther large sums of money for any amount of sleeping space available. Josiah marked off the rented spaces with stones he gathered for the purpose. Despite the cold winter winds, even the flat roof of the inn had been partitioned off into sleeping areas for travelers from distant cities.

It was late at night and Josiah returned to the storage room and told Esther, "That's it. There is not another square of space. Anyone else who comes will just have to be turned away. We've people in the dining area, people on the roof, and the entire courtyard is full of people and animals. There is no more room at …"

His words were interrupted by a knocking on the gate of the inn.

"Oh, no, not another," sighed Josiah.

He got up and went to the gate. Esther heard his voice, the negative tone indicating that he was telling another wayfarer that the inn was full. Although she couldn't hear the words she heard the pleading tone of the man who wanted into the inn's protective courtyard. Again, Esther heard the negative and apologetic tone of Josiah's voice, and then she heard the gate close.

"That was a sad one," said Josiah, when he returned to Esther's side.

"That poor man looked so tired and weary, and his young wife appeared to be about to have a baby any moment. But, what are we to do?

"A baby? You say the woman is about to have a baby, Josiah?" said Esther. "Well then we've got to do something! Surely there is some place we can put them. A woman can't have a baby by the side of the road."

"Esther, what can I do? I am not responsible for saving every man, woman and child from the circumstances this world has brought us to this night," said Josiah. The only thing I could have done would have been to take their donkey and put it in the stable."

"That's it, Josiah!" squealed Esther.

"Quick, you go and clean out the stable. Put down fresh straw. I'll run and tell the couple to return. They can stay in the stable. That is a better place for a baby to be born than by the roadside."

As she ran out of the storage room, Esther reached, with her good left arm, for a new blanket she had woven and saved for a special occasion. She tucked the blanket under her arm as she reached for the gate latch. Throwing open the gate, Esther ran into the roadway, looking first in one direction and then in the other, hoping that she could look through the dark night to see the couple Josiah had turned away from the inn. As she peered into the distance, a bright light suddenly appeared from the sky above. The light was so bright it caused Esther to look upward, and she saw in the sky a brilliant star, such as she had never seen before. Following with her eyes the beam of light from the star, Esther beheld the couple, the man walking, holding onto a tether which was tied to a halter attached to a donkey; seated on the donkey was a woman.

"People! You with the donkey," cried Esther, "come back, come back, there is a place where you can stay."

The man paused and turned, hardly believing what he heard. "Us?" he said, "Are you calling to us?"

"Yes," said Esther, "return to our inn, we've thought of a place where you can stay."

The man turned the donkey, and his steps quickened as though he thought if he didn't get to the gate quickly enough Esther would change her mind, or another traveler would take the offered space.

"I've money," he said, as he held out some coins.

"Oh, we'll take no money for this space," said Esther, then she led the man and the donkey across the courtyard of the inn. As was the custom, in the hill towns of Judea, the stable was the front part of a large cave next to which the inn had been built. Josiah had finished sweeping out the stable and had put a good supply of fresh hay over the old hay that was on the stable floor. He had even put a load of fresh hay in the manger after he had cleared out the remains of the feed from its bottom.

Esther put her blanket over the hay on the floor, while the man, who introduced himself as Joseph and his lady as Mary, carried the young woman and laid her on the blanket. Mary moaned a little as she was laid down, and it took only one look for Esther to realize that the baby was about to be born.

"Josiah, get some water and heat it on the fire."

"Joseph, go and take care of your donkey. I'll take care of your Mary and the baby," said Esther.

The men cleared out of the way, and Esther knelt down by the woman.

"Now, dear, take some short, quick breaths and push."

"There, now do it again. Oh, the baby is coming! Here it comes, oh, push a bit more. Harder now!

"Oh, it's a boy."

Fearing that she might drop the boy, Esther pulled her withered right arm out from her robe and steadied the baby's head with her little right hand.

"There you go." Esther patted the baby's bottom until he gulped in air, began to breathe and cry, too.

"Oh, a handsome boy," said Esther as she turned him right side up.

"There! Now you can hold him," said Esther, and she placed the boy in his mother's arms.

By the time she had finished caring for Mary, Esther saw that Josiah had brought a bucket of warm water and placed it by the stable entrance. Mary indicated a bundle which she had dropped on the floor just before Joseph had placed her on the hay. Esther brought the bundle to Mary, and she and the young mother together bathed the child. Mary took some new swaddling clothes, from the bundle, and with Esther's help wrapped them around the little boy. The two women decided that the manger, with its clean, sweet smelling hay was just the right size in which to place the child. Mary laid him there, and then she fell back upon her bed of hay. Esther knew she should go and get Joseph, so that he could see the new born babe. But first she had to look upon the child once more.

As she looked down at the baby, Esther said this prayer, "Oh God, protect this boy. Be with him at all times, and may he grow to know you and to live his life as you would have him live it. Amen."

When Esther whispered the final words of her prayer, the child's eyes opened, and looking into his eyes Esther had no doubt that her prayer would be answered. Then the baby's arms and feet began to move and he turned and twisted so that his coverings were kicked aside. Clucking her surprise over the strength in this new born child, Esther reached out to re-wrap the swaddling clothes. She was unable to lift the child and wrap the cloths with one arm, so she again pulled her right arm out from its hiding place, and tucked the cloth around the little boy's body. When Esther stood up, to go and tell Joseph that a son was born, she began to tuck her right arm back inside her robe. It was then that she realized her right arm was suddenly as straight and as healthy as was her left arm.

****

That, dear ones, is the legend of the innkeeper's wife. Her children, born late in life and healthy, every one of them, and her grandchildren, and their grandchildren, down through all the centuries, have told this story every year on Christmas Eve, which is why I have read it to you this night.

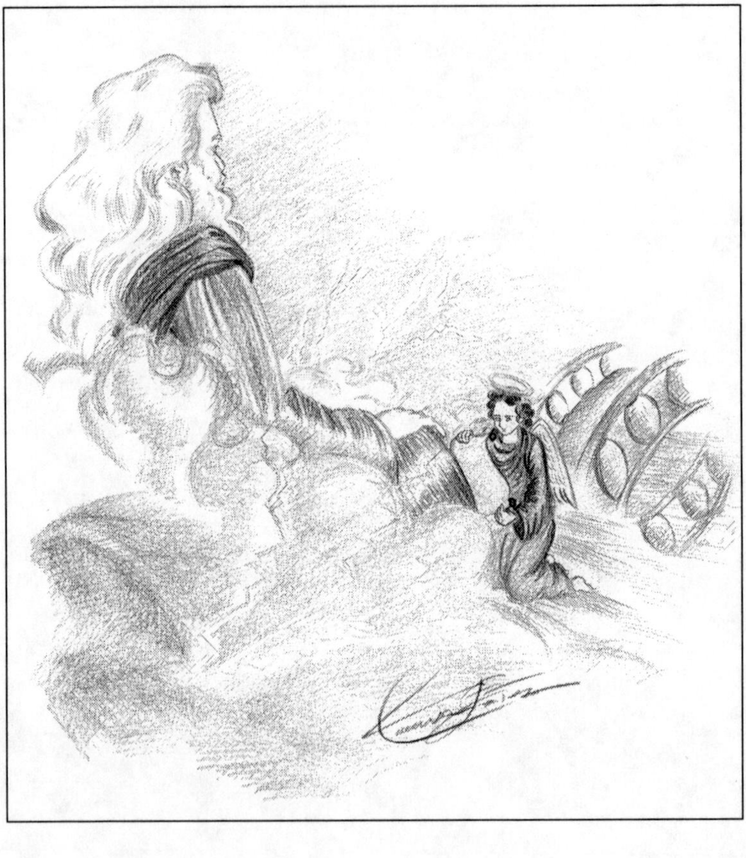

Tobel, An Angel's Story

Tobel is an angel. He is an angel who always tries to do what is good and right. Tobel always wants to say and do things that would be of benefit to others. Tobel always wants to delight the Lord God.

Eons ago, when Satan led many of the angels in a rebellion against the Lord God, Tobel did not follow Satan. He knew that what Satan was doing was wrong and Tobel had nothing to do with Satan.

Tobel is not the strongest angel, nor is he the smartest of the angels. Tobel also is not the handsomest of the angels. Tobel is just an ordinary angel who loves the Lord God with all of his being.

In fact, Tobel loves the Lord God so much that he always has wanted to do a great work for the Lord. But the opportunity has never presented itself to Tobel.

One day, hundreds and hundreds of years ago, as we count the years, the angels came to present themselves before the Lord.

The Lord God said, "I need one of you to go to the earth to speak to a young slave woman named Hagar. She must be told to be submissive to her mistress. Also, she is to be told that she will soon bare a son and that one day her descendants will be more numerous than one can count. Which of you will take this message for me?"

Tobel immediately raised his hand, as did almost all of the other angels. The Lord God pointed to an angel standing closest to his throne and that angel was sent off to earth on the mission.

On another day the angels came to present themselves before the Lord.

The Lord God said, "I need two of you to visit the earth with me. There is a man named Abraham whom I must visit. I need to let Abraham and his wife Sarah know that they are going to have a child, even though, by earth years, they are old beyond the time of child bearing."

"Oh," thought Tobel, "here is another opportunity to give news to someone. To go on a mission with the Lord God would be such a wonderful thing to do." Immediately Tobel raised his hand, but the Lord God didn't choose Tobel, he took two others angels with him on the mission.

Not long after that, several years on earth but only a moment in Heaven's time, the Lord God again asked for a volunteer to help the woman, Hagar. "She and her son have been put out of their home, and they are wandering in the desert wilderness. Both she and her son are perishing with thirst," explained the Lord God.

"I hear the boy crying out in his thirst," said the Lord God. "My messenger needs to show Hagar that a well is nearby"

Tobel raised his hand, he waved his arm back and forth, wanting so much to be of help to the Lord, but another angel was sent on this mission, too. Tobel became jealous of that angel.

Still another time, the angels presented themselves to the Lord and the Lord God said to them, "I have asked my servant Abraham to sacrifice his son Isaac. However, I do not want the child killed; I need one of you to call out to Abraham to keep him from slaying the boy. One of you with a strong voice will be the one to call out to Abraham"

Now Tobel had a strong voice and he was sure that he would be the one to call out to Abraham, but the Lord God chose another angel, not Tobel. Tobel was so disappointed and he became jealous of that angel, too.

There were many times as the earthly centuries passed when Tobel raised his hand and volunteered to go on missions to earth. However, Tobel was never chosen. As the years passed on Earth, the moments passed in Heaven, and Tobel became discouraged. He loved God so much but he also envied the angels who went to earth to do God's work. So, Tobel decided to speak with the Lord God to find out why he was never allowed to serve as one of the Lord's special messengers.

In Heaven, one doesn't just walk up to the Lord God's throne and begin speaking. There are so many people and angels in Heaven and it is very important for order to be kept in Heaven. So, there are certain procedures that even an angel must follow when he wants to speak directly to the Lord God.

Tobel followed all the procedures, and eventually he was notified that the Lord God would see him on the fourth Tuesday of the seventh month of the year, which on the Jewish calendar would be the month of Tishra; on a modern secular calendar, it is the month of July. Tobel made sure his wings were clean. He shined his halo better than he had ever shined it. He took with him a list of the times he had unsuccessfully volunteered for earth missions.

As Tobel neared the throne of God, his palms began to perspire. He wiped them on his robe and then hoped that no smudges would appear. The throne of God was most imposing. There was a rainbow which resembled emeralds that surrounded the throne. Flashes of lightning kept shooting out from the midst of the throne along with the sound of rumblings and peals of thunder.

All sorts of living creatures were around the throne. One looked like a lion, another like an ox, the third had the face of a man and the fourth was like an eagle. There were twenty-four other thrones that surrounded the Lord God's throne. Twenty-four white haired men wearing white robes sat on those thrones. There was a sea of glass that was crystal clear which Tobel had to cross to reach the throne. Tobel wandered how he would cross the Crystal Sea when suddenly a bridge appeared and Tobel knew that it was for his use.

Tobel kept his eyes down, sheltering them from the bright light which came from the Lord God. When he saw that he had reached the foot of the throne, Tobel knelt down and waited for the Lord God to speak.

"Tobel," the Lord God said, "I hear that you are upset about something. Read to me from the list you have brought with you."

"Oh, Lord God," said Tobel, "please believe that I have made this list not to upset you but so that I might remember all the times I've wanted to go on a mission for you and never got to go. I pray, Lord God, that you will not be upset with me. Please, Lord God, just know that I want to do work for you and I keep raising my hand and it's as though you never see me, and so I'm just here, Lord God, so that you will know who I am and that I love you, Lord God."

"Tobel," said the Lord God, "read from your list."

Tobel opened his list.

"These are times that I recall when I wanted to serve the Lord God and other angels were chosen but I was not chosen," read Tobel in a rather shaky voice.

"(1) there was the time when Jacob needed to be told about the streaked, speckled and spotted flocks. (2) I really wanted to be the angel who would go ahead of Moses and the children of Israel to guard them and bring them to the Promised Land. (3) It would have been so much fun to have been the angel who stood on the road to stop Balaam when he was riding his donkey. I would have loved to have seen the expression on Balaam's face when the donkey spoke in human words. (4) I volunteered to go to Gideon when he was threshing wheat, but I did not get to go on that mission either. (5) Because I want to do good and to deliver good news, I wanted to tell Zorah's wife that she would have a son, the boy named Samson. (6) It would have been such an honor to have been the angel who brought food to Elijah, but that honor also was denied me. (7) I could have helped Shadrach, Meshach and Abednego when they were thrown into the furnace and I was willing to be with Daniel when he was thrown into the lion's den. But those jobs also were not given to me. (8) Although war is not my strong point, I volunteered to go to help the angel who was delayed by the forces of evil when he had been sent to speak with Daniel who was at prayer for his countrymen. It was Michael who was chosen for that mission. Of course Michael is an archangel, and I understand that an archangel was a better choice for that particular mission. I wish I were an archangel so I could have gone instead of Michael. (9) On more than one occasion angels were sent to the prophet Zechariah.

I was never chosen for those missions, although I raised my hand each time."

Folding his list and holding it behind his back, Tobel then said, "There were many other missions to earth; too many to recall, Lord God. Please know that I am not being disrespectful, Lord God. I just want to serve you. Why do you always pick other angels and never me? My voice is strong. I am not afraid of the evil forces and I want to do something for you, Lord God."

"Tobel, Tobel," the Lord God said, "You are one who always and forever has wanted to do good in service to me. I've seen you raise your hand. At times you have even pushed ahead of the other angels in your eagerness to serve me. I know that you are so anxious to do good for me that you even are jealous of the angels whom I have sent on missions. Tobel, I've noticed you. There were other times, which you have forgotten, that you left off your list. But, I know of each and every time."

"Tobel, you are not yet ready to go on a mission. When you are ready, I will call on you." said the Lord God. With these words, the Lord God dismissed Tobel.

Time passed in Heaven. Often the angels presented themselves before the Lord. Tobel raised his hand each time the Lord God asked for a volunteer to go on a mission to earth. Each time other angels were chosen for the missions.

Tobel was especially disappointed when he was not asked to appear in the Temple to tell the man, Zechariah, that Elizabeth, his barren wife, would have a child. 'That would have been such good news to deliver,' thought Tobel.

One heavenly nano-second later, which was about six months of earth time, another angel was sent to the town of Nazareth to tell Mary, a virgin, that she was to have the holy child, the son of the Lord God almighty. That mission also was not given to Tobel; nor was Tobel chosen to appear in a dream of the man Joseph, who was to be the earthly father of the holy child.

After these assignments were given out, Tobel's disappointment was so great that he decided that he would never again raise his hand to volunteer for a mission. He decided that he would never be ready to go on a mission and that the Lord would never recognize him. Tobel was sure it was not in God's will for a lowly, ordinary, not strong and not very smart angel to serve the Lord God on a special mission.

Then Tobel became a very quiet angel. When the angels presented themselves before the Lord, Tobel never raised his hand. He also stopped envying the other angels. Tobel prayed that he might always do his best in whatever work in Heaven was assigned to him. It was then, in his prayer, that Tobel said that he was sorry that he had been jealous of the other angels. He also prayed that he might be good and loving to all the angels and all the people.

Just as he finished that prayer, Tobel heard the Lord God call his name.

"Yes, Lord," said Tobel.

"Tobel," the Lord God said, "I heard you ask forgiveness for the jealous thoughts that you have had for so long. Now that you have promised to not be envious of others, you are ready to go on a mission for me. You are to go to the earth, to a field outside the little town of Bethlehem. There you will find some shepherds guarding their flocks of sheep. You are to tell them the good news about the birth of my son."

That very moment... it was both an earthly and a heavenly moment... a quite delighted Tobel went from Heaven to Earth. Tobel went directly to the field outside the little town of Bethlehem, where he saw the shepherds, and then Tobel delivered the Lord God's message.

Tobel said to the shepherds, "Do not be afraid, for behold I bring you good news. That will be a great joy for all people. Today the savior was born. The one who is the called the Messiah, the Christ. He was born in the city of David, and this is how you will know him; he is wrapped in the cloths of a newborn baby and he is lying in a manger."

Suddenly Tobel was surrounded by many, many more angels. They were all praising God and saying, "Glory in the highest places to God, and on earth peace to all persons. Good will has come to all persons."

The mission was accomplished and Tobel returned to Heaven, where he was immediately summoned before the throne of the Lord God. Tobel was not scared this time when he crossed the bridge over the Crystal Sea and bowed down before the Lord God.

And, the Lord God said, "Well done, Tobel, my good and faithful angel."

And all of the angels in heaven said, "Amen, and Amen."

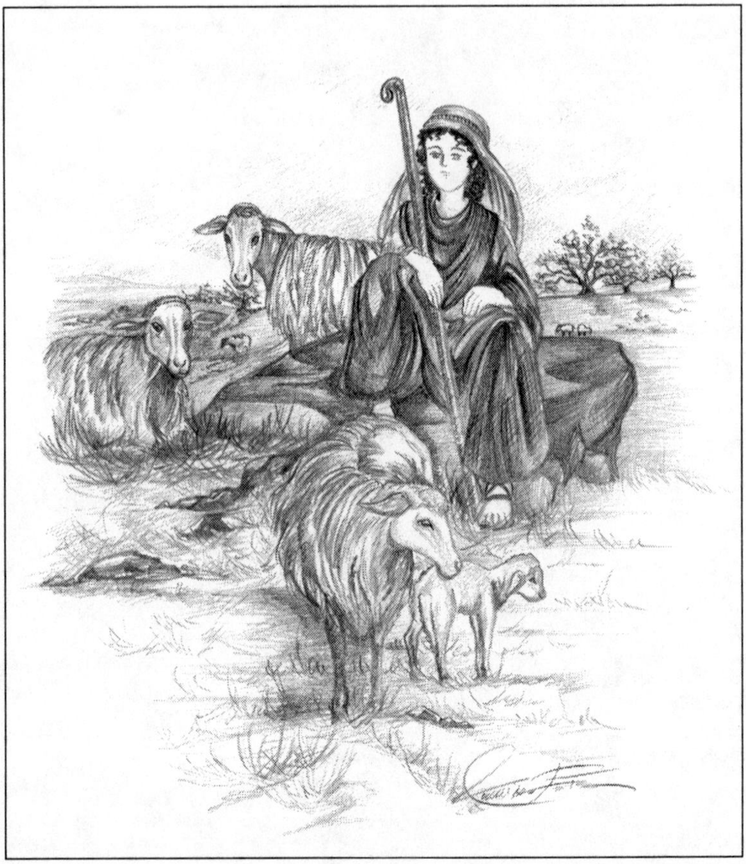

Samuel, A Shepherd's Tale

His name was Samuel, and he was a shepherd. Along with his family, he roamed the fields and pastures of the Promised Land, guiding and guarding the sheep that they might be led through the land to lush places for food, and yet always be safe from the harm which could come to them through the ravages of a hungry wolf or the crags and crevices of the rough places so close to the paths they walked.

Samuel was twelve years old, and he was a shepherd because his father was a shepherd, and before him, back as many generations as his father knew, the family had lived a wandering way of life, leading sheep. Samuel had eleven older brothers. Some of the brothers had left the shepherd's life and settled down in some of the cities of the land, taking up trades which would keep them in one place for all their lives. Samuel often wondered how those older brothers and their families could abide being in one place all the time. Samuel loved the wandering life and vowed that he would follow in his father's footsteps, following the weather and the water ways looking for the best places to which he could lead a flock of sheep, so that they might always find the best food and the purest water.

Water was most important to Samuel and his family. The sheep could not go for more than three or four days without water. Because of this, Samuel's family needed to know where the best wells and watering spots were located. Samuel's father also taught him that it was important to know who owned the wells and watering spots, for permission always had to be gained before the sheep could be watered.

In some areas, there were farmers who offered water and encouraged the shepherds to come onto their fields right after harvest time, so that the sheep could glean the good forage still available. While they grazed, the sheep would also naturally fertilize the fields, and their hoofs would break up the clods of dirt, thus helping the farmers to ready their fields for the next planting season.

It was the month of Tevet, and the celebration of Hanukkah had just past. Samuel's family had visited with two of his city-living brothers during the holidays. The brothers, after they had married, had settled in Jerusalem. One brother roamed the countryside each day buying the products of various farmers' fields, bringing those products to the sales booth his other brother had set up just outside the Damascus gate of the city of Jerusalem.

Following the celebration of Hanukkah, Samuel's father had moved his flocks a few miles south of the city, near a small town called Bethlehem. The fields near Bethlehem were fertile and the owners of those fields had been friends to Samuel's family for generations. So, the family tents were set up near the town, and Samuel, his father, and the remaining older brothers planned on keeping their flocks near Bethlehem through the rest of the month of Tevet, and through Shevat and most of the month of Adar. "After the celebration of Purim, we will head to the hills of Tekoa," Samuel's father had said. "Where we will meet with the descendants of our cousin Amoz.

Samuel was excited to be eventually going to Tekoa, his favorite cousin, Caleb, lived in Tekoa. Caleb was exactly Samuel's age, both of them having been born on the same day. So it was that one night, in a field near Bethlehem, while Samuel and several of his brothers were watching their flocks of sheep, that Samuel also was thinking about the fun he would have with Caleb. They would climb trees together, race over the fields together, and Samuel was sure that this year he would be able to hurl a stone with his slingshot farther than Caleb had ever thought of hurling one.

Earlier that evening Joshua, the oldest of Samuel's brothers, had pointed out to the brothers something strange which he had noticed in the sky. A new star seemed to have suddenly appeared. The star was brighter than all the other stars, and it seemed to hover over the town of Bethlehem. The star was quite big and bright. Samuel almost felt as though he could reach out and touch it. He wandered if his brothers, in Jerusalem, could see the star, and could Caleb, up in Tekoa, see it also?

Samuel's brothers discussed the star for some time. Did it bode good or evil for them? Was it a sign of bad weather coming, or did it mean that the rains would come as needed and the grasses would grow abundantly during the coming season?

Samuel and his brothers took turns sleeping, so that there were always several of them awake watching the flocks and on the lookout for robbers, who would not hesitate to steal a sheep or two. Like all shepherds, they also were aware that leopards, jackals, bears, and occasionally a hyena might want to fill its belly with a fresh lamb supper.

Samuel had just awakened his brother, Michael, and was folding his own robe about himself, preparing to lie down and sleep, when suddenly the sky was filled with a light that was brighter than any light Samuel had ever seen in his life. The light was not like light from the sun, which brought heat with its great light. This light did not heat up the land. The light was not like light from the moon which made everything glaringly white with black shadows looming upon the ground.

The light which caused the sleepy Samuel to open his eyes wide was warm, but not hot. It was brighter than the sun, but this light did not cause Samuel's eyes to hurt as he looked directly at it. It was not a white light, like the stars, but it was as though all the stars in heaven had suddenly come together with the moon and the sun. The light frightened Samuel.

Then, just as suddenly as the light had appeared, a voice seemed to come from the light, and Samuel saw a figure in the middle of the light. The voice, Samuel realized, came from the mouth of the figure he saw. The voice said, "Do not fear! Behold, for I give good news to you. It is news of great joy which shall be to all the people. Because, born to you today, in the city of David, is a savior, who is Christ, the Lord. And this to you is the sign. You will find a babe having been wrapped in swaddling clothes, lying in a manger.

Although Samuel had never seen an angel, he had heard about them. The Scriptures, by which his Father had taught him to read, had described angels; messengers from God. So, by the time the voice ceased speaking, Samuel had decided that the figure had to be an angel, sent by God. Then, suddenly there was, in the sky, a multitude of figures similar to the messenger, and Samuel cried aloud, "They must be angels." At the same time he heard his brothers saying, "Angels, angels from God." Then the heavenly messengers began praising God and saying, "Glory in the highest to God, and on earth peace in men, good will."

Samuel and his brothers all reacted differently. Matthew began to shout and sing; "Hallelujah! And Glory to God" he sang. A few of the brothers fell down on their knees and wept. Samuel was too astonished to do anything but continue looking up, and then as suddenly as the light and the angels had appeared, they disappeared. With the light gone, Joseph, who was always the more practical of the brothers, immediately turned his thoughts to matters at hand, which was the care of the sheep. He expected the sheep to be running all over the place. Sheep, which are not the smartest of animals, when frightened, will run and jump on top of one another, and will try to leap over rocks that are far too big for small legs to hurdle. Imagine Joseph's astonishment when he saw that the sheep had not been affected by the light, the voices, and the songs of the angels.

This to Joseph was more of a sign that God had sent the messengers, then even the words the messengers had spoken. So, Joseph turned to his brothers and said, "Let us go indeed unto Bethlehem, and let us see this thing that has occurred, which God has made known to us."

So Samuel, and his brothers, Michael, Matthew, and Joseph, left their flock of sheep, and hurried into the city of Bethlehem. Samuel saw that Joseph kept glancing at the big star which the brothers had noticed earlier in the night. As they neared the city, Joseph turn toward where the star was hovering, and Samuel realized that his brother was following the star. Joseph soon led his brothers into the courtyard of an inn, and as they crossed the courtyard, they saw that the light from the star was centered on the hillside cave next to which the inn had been built.

The cave, like so many near Bethlehem, was used by the innkeeper as a stable for his animals and for the animals of the guests of the inn.

Then Samuel's eyes beheld the manger, and there in the manger, just as the angel had said, was a baby wrapped in swaddling clothes. Near the manger was a young woman, who was leaning back into the protective arms of a man. But, it was not the man or the woman whom Samuel looked at long. It was the child, the child lying in the manger, who caught Samuel's attention.

Samuel had several nephews and nieces, and he had seen many new born babies, but never had he seen a baby quite like this one. Samuel fell upon his knees as close to the manger as he could get. He noticed that his brothers also had bowed down near the manger.

Samuel didn't know why he felt like worshipping this child; this new born baby. But, a feeling of worship and adoration swept over him. In later years, Samuel would say, to all who would listen, "There I was, and there were Michael, and Joseph, Joshua, and Matthew, all of us bowing down before this little baby. And, we wept, not in sorrow, but in joy. Oh, we felt a joy which we had never felt before. All because we saw a baby, wrapped in swaddling clothes, and lying in a manger. Finally, when we could tear ourselves away we left the stable and went out toward the fields and the sheep, and we began singing and praising God for all this which we had heard and seen that night."

148

Simeon, A Story of Faith

I, Simeon, a merchant and owner of many weaving looms in the garment district of Jerusalem, am putting pen to parchment because today there was a strange thing that happened during my morning time of prayer at the Temple. As I often do, many of my prayers end with the words, "Come Messiah. Please come, Messiah." This prayer is, I know, common to many of my people. For centuries the prophets told us that Messiah would come. However, almost four hundred years have passed since any prophet has spoken to us. God has been silent for so long.

There is so much crime, so much injustice. We are a people conquered and mostly ruled by gentiles, the Romans. A Jew is called king and does rule as such, a Herod, who has been king for at least twenty years. But, Herod seems to be concerned only with building plans. He is even rebuilding the Temple. Fortunately his builders work in such a manner that we can still worship in the Temple even as the new walls are being constructed.

Herod hasn't stopped the crime. Sin is rampant in our land. We are taxed too much and the tax collectors, even some of them are Jews, work for the Romans. There are factions within the leaders of our faith; they disagree on what the scriptures mean. They argue. There are those who use the Temple grounds for profit, by selling the birds and animals of sacrifice for greater fees than are just. And so, I pray, "Come Messiah. Please come, Messiah."

The strange occurrence was a voice that I heard as I prayed. I thought it was someone behind me.

I looked; no one was there. I looked to my right. I looked to my left. No one was near me. I heard the voice. It was clear and I will remember the words always, "Messiah will come and you will see him."

This was such a strange happening that I have decided to keep it to myself for the time being. Some persons, even my own sons, might think I have lost my mind, if I tell them I am hearing voices when no one is nearby to speak to me. I feel, though, that I should write this down and secured this parchment for that purpose.

******

Many months have passed since I first wrote on these parchments. I had nothing to write. Messiah has not come. But, today I again heard the voice. This time it was during the prayers I offer at noon. Again I had said, "Come Messiah. Messiah, please come." The voice spoke and the words I heard were,

"Messiah will come and you will see him here in the Temple."

No one was behind me or to my left or right. So, I said, "Who are you? Where are you?" There was no answer. I should have asked when this will happen. I am not a young man, any more. I wonder if I will truly live long enough to see Messiah.

How will I know that I have seen Messiah? The prophets spoke and wrote about Messiah's coming. Will I know Messiah by his name? Isaiah said that Messiah would have several names; such as Wonderful, Counselor, Emmanuel, and Prince of Peace.

Isaiah also wrote that Messiah would be born of a virgin. Surely when a virgin expects a child, it would be known throughout the land. God himself would have to protect that virgin because when it is realized that a single young woman, supposedly a virgin, is expecting a child, that young woman has to be stoned to death. That is the Law.

Micah, the prophet, wrote in our sacred scriptures that Messiah would be born in Bethlehem, a little town not too far from Jerusalem. How, in such a little town, could a young woman or her family conceal such a condition. But, would the family even know? Would they hide the woman? Wouldn't someone from the family want to tell the world that their family has been honored to bring Messiah to our people?

I don't have the answers to these questions. All I can do is pray. And, so I pray, Come Messiah. Messiah, please come.

****

Several years have passed since I first heard the voice. I have waited and wanted to hear the voice again or, at least, to have some sign. It's been so long now that I sometimes wonder if I imagined the voice because I so want to see Messiah. All of my life I have observed the Law, praying each day at the prescribed times, attending Temple more often than weekly and observing all of the High Holy Days. Now I find myself in continuous prayer. All of my children are grown and taking care of their families. My dear wife passed from this life a few years ago. Since my weaving business provides an income that supports my needs, I don't have to toil for my support. I want to be in the Temple morning, noon, and in the evenings, too. I am grateful to God that I am able to spend these final years of my life in daily, even hourly, worship.

Often, at the Temple, I feel as though God himself has wrapped his arms around me. I feel that God has come upon me. I feel lifted up in my spirit and it is an awesome feeling. Perhaps that is what the voice meant. Perhaps Messiah is a feeling, not an actuality. No, no, that can't be it.

There are two young men with whom I have conversed lately. In years past the father of one of them, a man from Aramethia, had been often a customer of mine, purchasing cloth for his family members and servants. The son of my late customer is called Joseph. The name of his friend is Nicodemus. These two young men have become like sons to me. We talk about the scriptures; especially do we discuss the prophecies concerning Messiah. I haven't told them about the voice, but I did share the fact that I sometimes wonder if Messiah is more a feeling than a real person who will come to us.

There is a woman who stays in the Temple night and day. Her name is Anna. I've heard that she is the daughter of Phanuel, of the tribe of Asher. Anna is a widow. Her husband died a mere seven years after their marriage. Anna never married again. She had three daughters and two sons whom she raised with the help of her own parents. After her children were grown, Anna came to Jerusalem, to the Temple, and she has never left it. Anna's sons followed Phanuel into business as merchants; the girls married well, raised their families and now enjoy their grandchildren.

When I go through the Court of the Women, I see the daughters of Anna visiting their mother. Daily they bring her food and care for her needs in every manner. They seem to do this quite willingly, for they say that their mother is a prophetess who has declared that she will live to see Messiah. Since Anna prays and fasts almost daily, her daughters have to urge her to eat the food they bring. Anna seems to live on the love of God alone, and she has done that for many, many years. I understand that she has seen more than eighty years of life.

I wonder if Anna has heard the voice. Should I discuss this with her? No, it would not be seemly of me to discuss such matters with a woman.

****

I invited Joseph of Aramethia and his friend, Nicodemus, to dine with me recently when I saw Joseph who was in Jerusalem for Passover. We had a private dinner and I was led to share with these two young men about the voice I had heard. It's been more than a dozen years since I first heard the voice. I've only heard it twice, I told my guests. Joseph and Nicodemus did not laugh at me or ridicule me. They listened and they prayed with me that I would hear the voice again and that I would see Messiah when he comes. Nicodemus lives here in Jerusalem. He is acquainted with Anna, the prophetess who stays always in the Temple, fasting and praying.

Nicodemus said he believes that Anna and I and he and Joseph will all live to see Messiah. That had best happen soon. Nicodemus, is a close friend of Anna's youngest son-in-law, and he told me that Anna recently passed the eightieth year since the day of her birth. I myself have seen more than seventy years pass in my lifetime. My body aches. My bowels do not work as they should. Most of my teeth are gone. I have shortness of breath. I doubt that I can live much longer upon this earth and I don't want my life to go on. If many more years must pass before Messiah comes, it is a surety that I will experience more and greater pain and the certainty of the loss of human dignity that comes with extreme old age. So, I pray. I pray, Come Messiah. Messiah, please come.

****

Almost two years have passed since I last wrote upon this parchment. Finally I have heard the voice again and what I heard was the very best of news. I was in the Temple at the evening time of prayer and now I continue to pray and to rejoice and praise the Lord God Almighty for the blessing the voice said that all Israel is to receive. The comforter, the very consolation and salvation of Israel is coming.

"Messiah is coming," the voice said. "Messiah will be here soon and you, Simeon, will know Messiah when you see him. He will be a babe in his mother's arms. The mother, a virgin, will give birth to this child in Bethlehem, although the mother and the man whom God has selected to be this baby's earthly father are from Nazareth. The mother and earthly father will bring the child to the Temple for the purification that is to be done according to the Law of Moses. The earthly father will purchase two doves or young pigeons and as they walk with the baby through the Temple courts, you Simeon, will see him. Simeon, you will not die from this life on earth until you see him, the one the Lord has appointed as Messiah."

Every day now I spend the major part of my waking hours in the Temple. I have bound myself, like a slave, to prayer and service for the Lord. Despite the pain, I lie prostrate before the doors that lead to the altar of incense which is just outside the Holy of Holies. In prayer I remain there for hours on end. Always I feel the loving arms of God touching me as I pray. I feel full of God and I rejoice in the Word which God has sent to me. Still I do pray, "Come Messiah. Messiah, please come."

****

This piece of parchment, which I purchased so many years ago, is almost filled with my writings. It surprises me not at all that I bought exactly the amount of parchment that I needed to make my notes. This is the last entry I will make. I leave this parchment to my oldest son to give to Joseph of Aramethia when he next visits Jerusalem. I believe Joseph will preserve these writings and share them with those who believe that Messiah has come, as I know it to be true.

Today, when I returned to the Temple for the noon prayer time, I was walking through the court of the Gentiles where I often spend time listening to the young teachers who gather there to teach and proselytize. My young friend, Nicodemus, was there; he is now a teacher of the Law. As I climbed the Temple stairs, I was so filled with a feeling of the nearness of God that I no longer felt any pain in my limbs. It seemed as though I floated rather than walked. Then I saw a young woman, holding a baby. She was accompanied by a man, who hovered protectively over the mother and child.

Once more the voice spoke to me. "That baby is Messiah. Just as I promised, you have lived to see the salvation of Israel. Take the child up in your arms. The mother will not mind." I did just as the voice instructed. I went to the parents and although the father was most protective, it was almost as though they expected to see me.

I took the child into my arms and looked upon his face. His hair was dark and curly. His skin, like mine, is slightly lighter than the color of the bark of an olive tree. But, it was his eyes which held my gaze. His eyes were not like those of other young babies, they were a deep dark brown and I had the feeling that he, looking into my eyes, could see into me, into the very depths of my soul. He eyes looked wise and kind and as old as time, although he is only an infant.

I thanked God, and blessed God, and my breath was restored so that I was able to sing this prayer.

"Now, Master, let your slave go in peace from this life, as you promised.

My eyes have seen the salvation you have prepared before the face of all the people;

a light for revelation to the nations, and the glory of your people, Israel."

I returned the baby to the arms of his mother. The parents began marveling at the prayer I had sung. I then blessed both parents and said to the mother, whose name is Mary, "Behold this child has been set aside by God for the spiritual fall or spiritual awakening of many in Israel, but his words, a sign to Israel, will be rejected. Yes, a sword will also pierce your soul, that the thoughts of many hearts may be revealed."

The voice told me what to say to the mother. It was not a message I totally understood, but the voice is of God and I had to give her that message.

Just before I left the Temple, Anna came. She is now at least eighty-four years of age. She moves slowly most of the time, but today, like me, she also moved as though she were floating. When she saw the baby Anna gave thanks to the Lord and witnessed to all who would listen that she had seen Messiah. She even went out into the city and spoke to all concerning the child.

That is my message. I now can lay down my pen, fold up this parchment, and lay me down to sleep, believing that the Lord God of All truly will allow me to enter Paradise this night.

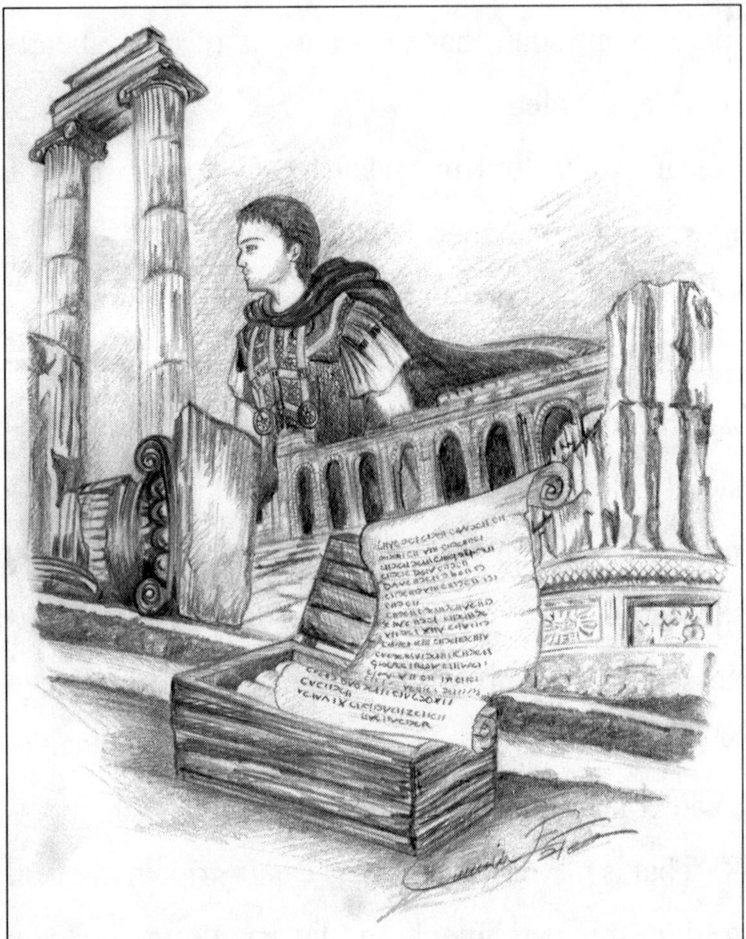

Letters Home, A Roman Story

*A*rcheologist digging recently in Rome discovered a hand carved wooden box which, for almost two thousand years, has survived time, progress, and new buildings constructed upon old foundations. Someone, long ago, wanting to protect the box had covered it with leather and surrounded it with bricks. Inside the box were several letters written on sheep's hide in the common language of those times, ancient Latin. Contemporary scholars have translated the letters into English. Here are passages from a few of those letters.

My dear Mother,

Justinion, a foot soldier in the legion attached to Palestine, and your loving son. Greetings to you and to my sister, Drucilla. I pray to the gods that this letter finds you in good health.

The corps to which I am assigned arrived in Jerusalem, after a stormy Mediterranean Sea voyage. We landed at the port of Caesarea, a man-made harbor which was constructed by our fine engineers several years ago, as you will recall. Also, you will be pleased to know that I suffered no illness from the sea and have so-far conducted myself with the honor you requested and which I pray would have been pleasing to my father whom the gods chose to wrench from your loving arms last year.

Shortly after arriving at our destination, various troops of our great 10th legion were sent into the country to different towns to keep the peace and control the crowds expected due to the census which our glorious Caesar Augustus has requested. I was posted to a town called Bethlehem.

A strange situation occurred earlier this evening which I observed and decided to report to you. I was on duty tonight outside a local inn. The inn was crowded, as is the entire town. The innkeeper was kind enough to bring me a bit of bread and meat for my evening meal. This was unusual because the natives here in Palestine, Jews as you know, resent our being here and do not usually offer us anything but sneers and, behind-our-backs, probably much worse.

I had just finished my dinner when a young couple approached the door to the inn. The man appeared to be about 10 years my senior but the woman, apparently his wife, seemed quite young, about the age of my dear sister, Drucilla, so the woman has not, I am sure, yet seen the second half of her second decade in life. The young woman looked ill and I could see that she was with child, even though she was on the back of a donkey and wearing long robes rather than the thinner, shorter garb a Roman citizen would wear.

The innkeeper apologized to the man. I have picked up enough of the local dialect to understand most of their conversations. There was no room at the inn for the man and woman. I heard the man explain that the woman was about to give birth. Still the innkeeper shook his head. There was no room, he said. The man turned the donkey around and began to leave the courtyard of the inn. Suddenly the innkeeper ran out to the gate, calling after the man, telling him that he might want to make the woman a bed in the stable. Curious, I followed as the innkeeper led the man around to the back of the inn.

Mother, this country is quite mountainous. Most of the out buildings in the countryside are built into the caves of the foothills. The stable to which the innkeeper led the man was one of those caves, and fairly large. The two men secured the animals outside the cave and placed some new straw in the manger. After fashioning a bed out of more straw and his cloak, the man helped the young woman off the donkey. I watched as the woman collapsed on the straw.

After seeing the couple settled in the stable, the innkeeper returned to his tasks at the inn and I returned to the courtyard area. I had previously noticed that it was a very dark night, so imagine my surprise, dear Mother, when suddenly the inn and the courtyard were bathed in a great light coming from a grand star which abruptly appeared in the sky above Bethlehem. Almost immediately after the star began to shine I heard the sound, though faint at first, of a baby crying in the night. I followed the sound which took me back to the stable where I saw the man and woman cleaning off the just born child, a boy. After he was washed, the woman wrapped the child in swaddling cloths and laid him in the manger. Again I returned to the front of the inn.

Not more than an hour later, through the gate of the inn came several shepherds. The innkeeper was getting water from the nearby well and the shepherds asked him if he had a stable and might a child have been born there. Wondering if the shepherds were there to cause trouble, I followed them to the stable where the innkeeper had directed them. It was amazing Mother. The shepherds knelt down and worshiped the child, just as you and I worship our household gods before the altar in our home. I heard them saying the word, Messiah, which I didn't and still don't really understand.

I am now off-duty and about to go to sleep. Since writing materials are scarce, it might be a long time before I again write you, Mother. Do ask the gods to protect me, as I ask them to take care of you. My tour here in Palestine will last almost three years, as you know. Pray that I return to Rome, to your love and care. But, I go where Caesar asks me to go and I serve as I am ordered.

Here in Bethlehem, the star I described is still shining. I wonder if it is shining on Rome, too.

Your loving son, Justinion

My Dear Mother,

Justinion, loyal cohort of the 10th legion, loyal subject of our great Caesar Augustus, brother of Drucilla, and loving son of you dear mother, Diana.

I've just come off-duty and wanted to put in writing my feelings about current events here in Palestine. This letter I will not send as usual, but am taking the precaution to send it with a brother-in-arms who has sympathies similar to mine.

Mother, do you recall that about two years ago I wrote to you shortly after I came off duty where I had been on watch at a local inn? The night that I wrote you there was a most unusual heavenly occurrence of a great star which lit up the night sky so that it was almost like day. That same night a child was born in the cave-like stable of that inn. The star continued to shine in this area, creating lots of comments for it was so unusual. No one was able to figure out what had caused the gods to change the sky so suddenly. Many were fearful of this new constellation.

Over the next few days, whenever I was on duty at the inn, I was surprised by the numbers of local persons who came to visit the family in the stable. You might remember that I had written that some local shepherds had come to see the child just hours after he was born. They referred to the child as "Messiah". I have learned that Messiah is a term from their holy books, apparently it is what they call an expected savior. Why any country would need a savior when the troops of Rome can protect them is beyond me.

Several days after the child was born, the man carried the woman and child to a home here in Bethlehem, where I have seen them at various times during the last twenty-plus months. Apparently the father is a carpenter who was able to secure work in the area.

The child is a handsome boy, dark of hair and eyes, like the people of this land. He doesn't resemble the man at all but is not really in the image of his mother, either. An ancient forefather has apparently left his mark on this boy. His mother seems quite shy. I have seen her at the local well when she goes for water. Before the boy learned to walk, the mother carried him on her hip while she balanced her water jug on her head, holding the child with one hand and the jug with the other. She has made friends with some of the women but she is quiet and doesn't join them in their times of gossip. Although the woman is a common Palestinian, she has a certain look about her such as I have never seen on the face of any other woman. It is a look quite calm, as though she has great thoughts which she ponders.

The great star that I mentioned had finally disappeared and was missed for a while so that eventually people stopped speaking of it. Then unexpectedly a few weeks ago the star again appeared. It came out when I was on duty in the residential quarter one night. It almost seemed to shine on the house of the boy's family, which is strange because when they were staying in the stable, months ago, it seemed the star hovered over that place, too.

I was again on duty in the residential area a few days later when a caravan of grandly dressed persons went to the boy's house. The camels in the caravan were well laden and one could tell that these were wealthy visitors, seeming like kings in their appearance and mannerisms. As guard of the area, it was my duty to be aware of what was going on. I stood near the house ready to stop any problems which might arise and disturb the peace but the man and the woman welcomed the strangers into their home. The visitors spoke with strange accents but I understood one of them to say that they were there to see the "King of the Jews." The king was not in that home, so these words greatly puzzled me.

The king of this area is Herod, who was granted his power by our great Caesar Augustus.

Watching, I saw the men offer the couple presents even before they entered the house. Within a short time, probably following a light meal, the strangers exited the home, immediately mounted their camels and set out from the town. I don't know who the men were but could tell, by their look and strange sounding language, that they were from some far off foreign land or lands.

Now, Mother, I come to the reason for this letter being written and sent as I mentioned above. A few days after the strangers left the area, King Herod ordered the death of all male children born in Bethlehem since the time the great star first appeared.

A few years ago when I became a foot soldier for Rome, I was trained as a soldier, ready for war to keep the peace. I was trained to obey the orders of my superior officers and have done so without thinking about it. But, I never thought I would be ordered to slaughter innocent babies who just happened to be born because the gods had sent a strange and brilliant constellation into the sky. It was horrible and for the first time in my life I regretted being a soldier. As my fellow foot soldiers and I went from street to street searching out the male children, questioning the families about the ages of the boys, I couldn't help but wonder about the boy who had been born in the stable.

I wondered if I could kill that boy. I knew I couldn't disobey my orders and I felt a constriction in my chest the closer we got to the street where the boy lived. Mother, I was relieved when we got to the boy's home and found it empty. As a matter-of-fact, the house looked as though the family had moved out. The shelves were empty and the cloth hooks bare. I haven't seen the father, the mother, or the boy since that time. I thank the gods for taking from me a decision I did not want to make; to kill the boy or to disobey my orders.

Blood came from many homes in Bethlehem during those days. I wash my hands of it. I was just obeying orders. The wails of the mothers and other family members will stay in my mind for many months. Such is the life of a soldier.

My love to you, dear Mother, and to my sister Drucilla. I will soon be home. You will be pleased to know that I have received a promotion and will be in Rome for special training in preparation for my next assignment.

Justinion, son and soldier.

There were several other letters in the box, but it is from the last two letters that I now read.

My dearest wife,

Justinion, loving husband, loyal Centurion in Caesar's 10th Legion. Greetings from Jerusalem. I pray to the gods that you and our children and grandchildren and my sister, Drucilla and her family, are all in good health.

One of my trusted soldiers will be returning home to Rome. He leaves in a few days and I have asked him to bring this letter to you.

I wanted to tell you about a man, by the name of Jesus, whom I heard speak recently. Jesus is from the region of Galilee, a town on a hilltop called Nazareth. They say he makes miracles and that he even heals people. I find that hard to believe but they say it is so. As a matter-of-fact, one of my friends, a fellow Centurion, claims that this miracle worker healed his servant without even seeing the servant who was ill to the point of death. My friend took me to hear this Jesus speak.

I was amazed at the words of Jesus. He spoke about love and doing good to all people. He told stories that encouraged people to even love their enemies. He said that all persons are equal in the eyes of his god. He said that his god was the only god and referred to him as his father in heaven.

I heard some of the people refer to this Jesus as the Messiah. Recall, dear wife, that many years ago I told you about my first posting to Palestine, when I was a mere foot soldier. That I was in Bethlehem and saw a baby born in a cave-like stable I told you that some shepherds referred to this boy as the Messiah. Now people say this Jesus is the Messiah. These Jews are always searching for and waiting for their Messiah. They say their Messiah will come and save them. They say the Messiah is the son of their god. This Jesus spoke well and I liked hearing his stories. But, I don't believe he is a Messiah, he could be more of a trouble-maker. At least his followers are making trouble, it seems.

Jesus came to Jerusalem a few days ago. Many of the people ran out to greet him. They picked branches from the palm trees and waved them, which is a sign of rebellion. The people had a great parade, almost like an army's victory parade. Some of the people even laid down their cloaks before the feet of the donkey on which Jesus was riding, as if he were a great general or king.

A few days later Jesus was in the courtyard of the Jewish temple and he drove out the venders who were selling the doves, rams, sheep and other items which the people buy to offer as sacrifices. Jesus acted furious, over-turning the tables of the money changers. This Jesus has stirred up the people and the leaders of the Jews are upset at him, too. He left the temple, escaping before the leaders could do anything about him. He left the city, too. I hope he doesn't return. He is a disturbance to the peace of this area and therefore to the peace of Rome. There is nothing more important than the peace of Rome.

I must sign off now, dear wife. Give the soldier who delivers this missive a meal and a handsome gift. I remember how it was to be a foot soldier, without any luxuries. This man is good and he deserves to be well treated.

In loyalty, first to Caesar and next to you, dearest Prisca, and our family, I am Justinion, proud to be a Centurion of Rome's Empire.

Dearest Wife,

I believe this letter will reach you before I arrive home. Does that surprise you? Yes, I am coming home. This old soldier is retiring. I've been loyal to Rome and her emperors and worshiped them as gods. I've been a good soldier for almost thirty-five years. But, events have occurred which have shaken me to my very soul, even as the earth was quaking here in Jerusalem twenty-four hours ago.

Very recently you should have received a letter from me, brought by one of my loyal foot soldiers. In that letter I told about a man called Jesus. I recall writing that he could bring a lot of trouble to this area.

Well, the trouble began the very evening that I wrote to you. I will fill you in on all the details when I arrive back in Rome. But, I realize that some explanation is necessary so that you might understand and prepare for my unexpected homecoming and retirement.

You see, dear wife, I have come to realize that my life's thoughts about the gods are wrong. I realize that teachings I received at my mother's knee were not truth. Oh, not that my mother lied, she just didn't know the truth. I also know, and if this letter falls into the wrong hands, it could mean my death, but I know that Caesar is not god. I now realize that no emperor is or ever will be god.

In my last letter I told you about a man named Jesus. Well, three nights ago, Jesus was arrested by the Jewish temple guard. Early in the morning, before dawn, he was brought to testify before the leaders of the temple. Then he was taken to the Roman Prefect, Pontius Pilate. Pilate ordered Jesus to be executed because he, or his followers, claimed that he, Jesus, was the king of the Jews. This day was a religious holy day for the Jews, a time they call Passover. Continuing a local tradition, Pilate offered to set one prisoner free. He offered the Jews, Jesus. They called for another rebellious man, one called Barabbas. Frankly, I and some of my fellows thought Barabbas by far the worse character, but Pilate had to do as the people demanded. It is tradition. And, Pilate was sure the peace would be broken if he went against the people's wishes. Keeping the peace is, of course, the primary consideration.

After the customary beatings and scourging, some of the soldiers, by now drunk with their own violence, fashioned a crown of thorns from branches of the Jujube tree. They pushed the crown down on Jesus' head until the blood dripped in a ring of red over his hair and into his ears and in his eyes. Stripped almost naked, Jesus was led into the street where the *patibulum*, or crossbar of the cross was placed on his back. We then led him out of the city to a hill called Golgotha, which is where the local crucifixions take place.

Jesus didn't carry the crossbar all the way up Golgotha. He stumbled and fell many times and I finally picked a man from the crowds along the way to finish carrying it. When we got to Golgotha, my soldiers began hammering long iron spikes into the hands and feet of Jesus and two thieves who were being crucified also. While the hammering was going on, the man who had carried the crossbar told me that he hardly felt the weight of his burden at all. That was strange indeed, dear wife. The crossbar weighs more than you and our youngest grandchild together might weigh.

Pilate had demanded that a notice be placed on the cross of Jesus which read, in three languages, "This was the King of the Jews." People always come to gawk and mock at those being crucified. Yesterday was no different, except even the priests from the temple and the local lawgivers came and mocked this Jesus.

Although the day had been clear, all of a sudden at the sixth hour, the skies turned curiously dark. It was frightening.

Jesus spoke very few times. Once he said that he was thirsty. One of the foot soldiers raised up to him a sponge filled with vinegar. We soldiers can be so cruel at times. I have seen joy on the face of other soldiers as they kill during war. I recall even the lack of remorse some of my fellow soldiers evidenced when we were commanded to murder many children in a little town here in this country about thirty years ago.

There was a time when Jesus spoke to a man and an older woman, one about the age of my sister, Drucilla. He said to them, "Dear woman, here is your son. Here is your Mother." The woman had a look about her that was strangely familiar to me, but at the time I couldn't recall where I might have seen her.

It was the ninth hour when Jesus cried out words in the Aramaic language, which I will never forget. In our language I write them to you, "My God, My God, why have you forsaken me." I looked at him at that moment and his entire countenance had changed. He had been a rather nice looking man, well built, with a face pleasant to behold. But at that moment, his face was haggard, scarred, and ugly. His body had broken out in every type of boil, wart, and pus-oozing blemish one can imagine. He was ugly and misshapen. He had a look such as I have only seen on the worst criminals. He looked like the most evil sinner of all sinners. The last words I heard from Jesus were, "Father, into your hands I commend my soul." Immediately the ground shook in the worst earthquake I have ever experienced. The earth split open and rocks fell apart. Buildings shook and I later learned that, in the Jewish temple, the curtain which hides their most holy place, was torn in two from top to bottom.

I was terrified and at that moment, I heard my own voice cry out, "Surely this man was the son of God." Dear wife, I believe what I said. I felt, deep within my heart, that I had spoken truth. When the earth finally quit shaking, I looked at Jesus and thought he was dead but still ordered one of my soldiers to thrust a spear through his side, just to be sure. Because I didn't move out of the way quickly enough, the blood and water which flowed from Jesus' side even covered me.

My life has changed dear wife. I leave early on the morrow for Rome. Soldiers from my company have been posted to guard the tomb of Jesus but I will leave Jerusalem before they come off duty.

Letters arrive home faster than do soldiers. I will leave from Caesarea, the very port at which I first arrived in this country three decades ago. I have to stop in Crete on my way home. But, within three months, I will be home with you. I will bring with me a copy of the Jewish scriptures which I am going to read many times because I believe they will lead me to an understanding of the God of the Jews and this man, Jesus, who surely was his son.

Love comes to you with this letter from your husband,
Justinion

Retired soldier
Centurion
and one who comes home to ponder all the thoughts that I have ever thought.

Post Script - I have just remembered where I had seen the woman, the one Jesus referred to as mother. She was much younger the last time I saw her, but she had about her a certain look which I recall even though more than thirty years have passed. It is a look, quite calm, but as though she has great thoughts upon which she ponders. That woman was the mother who gave birth to the little boy in the stable of the inn one night when I was on guard duty in the little town of Bethlehem.